ENERGY HEALING

FOR

EVERYONE

ENERGY HEALING

FOR

EVERYONE

A Path To Wholeness
and Awakening

Brett Bevell

Monkfish Book Publishing Company
Rhinebeck, NY

Library of Congress Control Number: 2014944124

Paperback ISBN: 978-1-939681-19-5
E-book ISBN: 978-1-939681-20-1

Printed in the United States of America

Book and cover design by Danielle Ferrara

Monkfish Book Publishing
22 E. Market St., Suite 304
Rhinebeck, NY 12572
www.monkfishpublishing.com

For Helema and the Eternal Light that
flows through her eyes.

Table of Contents

Introduction

Energy healing is for everyone, because it is inexpensive, universal, and unlimited. It can effect positive change for anyone on the physical, emotional, and spiritual levels. It can release stress, or—as Chinese medicine has known for centuries through acupuncture—restore vitality and balance to organs and systems of the body. It can be used to clear negativity from a situation, as is often taught in the very popular form of energy healing known as Reiki. There are even some energy healing modalities that can address karmic conditioning from past lives, allowing one to move beyond cycles of dysfunction and disease in ways that modern medicine and modern psychology cannot touch.

We are all made of energy. Einstein knew this when writing his famous formula $E=MC^2$, which in layman's terms simply says that everything is made of energy, even matter, which is simply energy in its most dense form. If everything is made of energy, including us, then everyone has the ability to be an energy healer and use energy healing to improve their daily lives.

There are many forms of energy healing, most of which can be traced to Eastern spiritual traditions. The origins of Reiki can be found in Japanese and Tibetan Buddhism. Chinese medicine and qi gong have their roots in the Taoist traditions of ancient China. Even the popular concepts of chakras and chakra healing, often taken for granted in some Western New Age healing modalities, have their roots in the Vedic texts from the Hindu spiritual tradition of India. These popular forms of energy healing have touched millions of people's lives in a profound way, causing an energy healing revolution that has empowered people all around the globe to take charge of their own personal well-being on the physical, emotional, and spiritual levels.

I have either personally witnessed or heard directly from those who have used energy healing techniques to overcome stress, anxiety, depression, the emotional scars of childhood sexual abuse, homelessness, and even some debilitating physical illnesses such as cancer. The true promise of energy healing is that it is absolutely free for those who are trained in it and unlimited in abundance: Because energy is what everything is made of.

I have great respect for the various forms of energy healing now available to all of humanity, and have dedicated my adult life to the study and research of many of these forms. Yet there is one form that is relatively unknown and has its roots in the first few lines of the Bible, where God spoke the universe into existence saying: *Let there be light!* This form of energy healing, much like Einstein's formula $E=MC^2$, relies on the basic fundamental principle that everything is made of light/energy. Yet this form of energy healing takes Einstein's formula one step further, by remembering that that light from which all creation is made comes from the Divine. This form of energy healing is called Light of the Eternal One.

Light of the Eternal One accesses the Divine energy field that is the basis for all creation. It is that fundamental light from which all things arise. The secret for accessing this light was revealed to me during a series of profound mystical experiences I had over a period of months during 2007. At that time in my life I had visions of complex mathematical equations that were beyond my ability to rationally comprehend, but which when contemplating them would open me to a euphoric sense of the eternity in all things. I felt guided by ascended masters, angels, directed by the prophet Ezekiel to rediscover what I was told was an ancient Essene energy healing practice called Light of the Eternal One.

The Essenes were a mystical, egalitarian, peace-oriented sect of Judaism that believed in the concept of a Mother/Father God. They existed during the time of Christ, and some psychics such as the late Edgar Cayce claim that Jesus, Mary, and her husband Joseph were Essenes. Some also attribute the writings of the Dead Sea Scrolls to the Essenes. Though I am not a historian and do not base my belief on historical text, I can say that this energy called Light of the Eternal One fits well with the egalitarian and peaceful nature of the Essenes.

Light of the Eternal One is energy healing for everyone. It has one primary hand position and is very easy to learn, as well as easy to teach and share with others. It works to promote a sense of inner peace, calm, and sometimes euphoria by dissolving those parts of human consciousness that keep us feeling separate and isolated from the Divine. By bridging our awareness back to a place of knowing we are one with the Divine, one with God, Light of the Eternal One restores us to our true sense of self, a place of spiritual sanity. And when living from this place of spiritual sanity, the deeper roots of our suffering and illness vanish. That is because these roots always exist in the illusion that we are not one with the Divine.

Stepping forward into the chapters that follow is like returning to the Garden of Eden. If you make a daily practice of using Light of the Eternal One on yourself, it is like bathing your mind in a light that continuously reminds you of your connection to the Divine. Anxieties, fears, and unwanted emotions will begin to fall away and be replaced by a sense of wholeness. You will be shown how to bless friends and family with this light, how to send this light distantly to others and to improve all aspects of your life, and how to teach Light of the Eternal One to everyone you may wish to share it with. For most, Light of the Eternal One is an extremely simple, powerful, and user-friendly form of energy healing that works to deepen our sense of wholeness and well-being by deepening our connection to the Divine. And for some, Light of the Eternal One can actually lead them to a place of spiritual awakening, where that sense of oneness with the Divine is continuous, never-ending, pervading one's consciousness without end.

$$\text{(I)}$$

Acknowledging the Light

A healing transmission of Light of the Eternal One has been sent across time and space to all who read this book. Please know that in reading any part of this book, you are engaging this blissful and sometimes euphoric light called Light of the Eternal One.

Light of the Eternal One is a Divine energy form that sustains all creation, including our universe. In the Bible it says that in order to create the universe, God first said, *Let there be light.* And it was only after this light emanated from the Divine that creation did appear. Regardless of your religious beliefs, even science views the universe as made of energy, or light, the quantum field that manifests things into existence. This light has always been there and has always been part of us. Now, as part the Divine plan of our human evolution and the accelerated spiritual development on this planet, this sacred light has been made available for all to access for the purpose of promoting healing and spiritual awakening.

This book is about *Us*. And I do not mean the small *us* in the way that word is used to denote two or more people as a couple or small group of friends. I mean the larger Us. The Us that is sacred and Divine. The Us that includes your consciousness and mine, and that greater being that some call God, Jesus, Buddha, Allah, Goddess, Krishna, Hanuman, Kwan Yin or myriad other names. I write this for the Us that includes both human and animal, both material and spirit, both individual and universal. We are all interconnected, and this book holds a special energetic secret, a secret longing to be discovered that both screams and whispers how interconnected and of the same being all of Us are.

This book is a doorway to remembering our true nature, which is Divine. If you decide to step forward into the cupped hands of this book, it will hold you. It will bless you and offer you a means for managing the madness of this age and turning that madness into a nectar that is sweet, never-ending, and eternal. For through this book has been sent a sacred, energetic empowerment of the Light of the Eternal One, an empowerment that is available to all who seek it.

Light of the Eternal One can be thought of as the energy that creates the Divine matrix, the field of God-presence that sustains the universe. If you allow its influence to bathe your consciousness, the possibility for life change toward the positive good is extreme. And that is the promise of this book: That it will open you to this energy in such a way that it can flow through you and be directed by you for healing, inner peace, and spiritual growth.

What will happen to you after working with this energy for a period of time may or may not be what the sages call enlightenment, for who can say exactly what enlightenment is? But what will happen for sure is a knowing of the deep interconnection between you and all things, all beings, a spiritual equivalent to a return to the Garden of Eden.

Turning on the Light

I have learned after studying a variety of energy healing modalities for over a decade that there are esoteric avenues for encoding and sending huge energy transmissions through words and words alone. These techniques are practiced and proven, and can be thought of as an energy download from the Divine computer, as if there was One mind to which we are all connected, as if we are computers plugged into the World Wide Web of Divine consciousness. I have found that just as you can access information on the Web by simply Googling the correct word or phrase, so too can you download Divine energy into your own system by invoking a phrase that has been intentionally encoded with that same Divine energy. It sounds too easy, but has been tested numerous times and works with 100 percent accuracy.

This chapter contains one such chant that will empower you to be able to flow Light of the Eternal One through your hands for the rest of your life. Unlike other energy traditions, wherein an exchange of energy is required from those who receive the empowerment, I have been told that such is not the case with Light of the Eternal One. Because the Divine so deeply loves witnessing the joy created when people access this energy, simply using this energy and thereby creating a more joyful world is the only energy exchange required. However, in keeping with the sacredness of this empowerment, it is recommended that you properly prepare yourself to receive this spiritual gift. Also know that in receiving this gift your energy system will be forever altered, which means you can very possibly experience significant life changes just from receiving the empowerment. Therefore, I recommend giving thought as to the day you will engage this life-changing energy. You may want to do it on a sacred day that is part of any spiritual tradition you might abide by, such as Easter, Passover, Solstice, or other such religious holiday from whatever tradition is in alignment with your own spiritual path. Or, you may want to engage this empowerment on a day that is in keeping with the power cycles of the moon, and choose to receive it when the moon is full and relishing in the bounty of the sun, or when it is new to inspire this new beginning. You may even decide to pick a more personal day, such as your birthday, an anniversary, or other significant date in your life. Pick a date that is meaningful to you and which is symbolic to the occasion.

When the day comes that you wish to engage the empowerment, properly prepare yourself for the empowerment you are going to receive. The primary preparation I recommend is a simple cleansing of your aura by taking a bath with an added pinch or two of sea salt. This sea-salt bath will cleanse away any negative energy that may be present in your aura. After soaking in the sea-salt bath, dress in a manner that for you suits the occasion of receiving this spiritual gift. Then, before engaging the empowerment chant, light a candle in honor of the Divine, invoking whatever name or names that you use to connect with the Creator. Meditate on this candle and think about the underlying Divine energy that supports all creation. Know that with the empowerment you are about to receive you will have the ability to call forth through your hands that Divine light that supports all creation, and use it to dissolve all illusions you may have of being separate from the Divine. You will come to understand when using this wonderful energy that the place where eternity begins is everywhere, and that no such place exists that is not part of the eternal equation of infinite creation. By using your hands to call forth this eternal light, you will heal many spiritual wounds for both yourself and others. After meditating on the candle, and contemplating your relationship to the Divine and the eternal presence that supports all creation, engage the empowerment chant by saying the following:

Blessed is all that is
Blessed is all that I am
I ask to be empowered with Light of the Eternal One
Blessings unto all
Blessings unto me

Be still and quiet and allow for the energetic empowerment to occur. Some people I have offered this empowerment to speak of feeling light-headed afterwards, or of feeling a sense of unrestrained happiness or bliss. Simply engage this empowerment without judgment, and notice how it makes you feel.

Once you have received the empowerment, use Light of the Eternal One on yourself as a short blessing by simply placing your hands on top of your head, asking to connect to the spiritually awakened beings, angels, devas, gods, and goddesses devoted to the process of spiritual awakening. Then ask these beings to allow this light to flow down from the heavens through your hands. You might even see something like a waterfall of white light coming down from above, into the center of your head, and through your hands. Hold your hands in this position for a few minutes, and notice any sensations of peace, bliss or euphoria that may arise as you allow this energy to flow into you. The ease and simplicity with which this energy works is astounding, and though more in-depth treatments using this energy will be explained in later chapters, you now have a simple spiritual tool that can never leave you and that brings joy to both you and the Divine the more you use it.

The Basic Treatment

The simple joy of Light of the Eternal One is that it works so easily anyone can learn it. Yet at the same time it has a powerful impact on all who receive this light. The real journey in using this energy is to make a daily practice of it.

Imagine how wonderful the world would be if each of us had the power to remember at any moment the Divine presence that created us, to remember this presence not just intellectually, but emotionally, spiritually, and even feel it physically through the cells of our body. Light of the Eternal One offers everyone this opportunity. The challenge is in using this wonderful light as a daily practice.

Since many of us are socially conditioned to feel we are unworthy of being connected to the Divine, it is not as easy as it may seem to allow yourself the joy of experiencing a daily treatment of a Divine energy that can bring you into a state of bliss and inner peace. That conditioning, however, can be overcome with the dedication and routine of creating a daily energy healing practice.

To begin your own journey with this practice, start by dedicating a particular time each day when you know you can give yourself a short Light of Eternal One treatment. This time can be either in the morning when you first wake up, in the evening before you go to bed, or at some other time of your convenience when you know you will consistently have time to yourself. The treatment itself is not long for this type of work, normally lasting approximately five minutes.

Once you have chosen your specific time frame for this work, commit to it. Within reason, do not let anything get in the way of your daily practice. You may want to mark this time on your calendar to make sure you don't forget it. Then, having made the commitment, follow the simple routine outlined below. I recommend doing so initially for forty continuous days without an interruption. You may find that once you commit to a forty-day cycle, integrating the routine into your life pattern will become relatively easy.

The Light of Eternal One basic treatment is very easy, and can be thought of less like an energy healing and more like an energetic communion with the Divine. Simply place your hands on top of your head as you did after first receiving the Light of Eternal One empowerment. Intend and allow the white, sparkling light to flow down from the heavens into your head. Even if you do not see or feel the energy, as some people do not feel subtle energies, keep with the routine anyway. For even if you are one of those people who may not feel the energy, you will still be affected by the treatment. Hold your hands on top of your head for at least five minutes. First, envision filling up your skull with this Divine light. Then, once you imagine your skull is full, envision the same sparkling white light traveling down your spinal cord into your entire nervous system. If you are one of those people who are energy sensitive, you may feel at a certain point like you have *filled up* with the energy. At that point you can release your hands from on top of your head and simply let your consciousness bathe in this wonderful presence of the Divine. If you are not one of those people who are sensitive to subtle energies, simply keep your hands on top of your head for the five-minute time period, which is sufficient to gain the desired effect on your consciousness and deepen your sense of oneness with the Divine.

Eventually, using this basic treatment over a period of time can lead your consciousness into the state the Hindu and Buddhist traditions refer to as *Samadhi*, a state where there is no sense of separation between you, the Divine, and all creation. That is the desired goal of this basic treatment, and a goal that most of you are likely to experience if you remain committed to the forty-day cycle.

Journaling the Forty-Day Cycle

You have just learned the basic treatment that is the core of the forty-day cycle. Now, accompanying that treatment with a simple journaling activity can help ground this energy into your life. I have found that in writing about your experience, it helps to honor that experience as well as provide a record of your journey.

For the next forty days, write at least a short paragraph each day about what you felt and experienced while you were receiving the treatment. This is best done right after receiving the treatment, as that is when your mind is still experiencing a direct energetic communion with the Divine. You may be surprised at the insights you can attain about your own life while writing, as journaling at this time causes you to expand this blissful sensation of communion and ground it into thoughtful reflection about your relationship to the Divine, yourself, and others. You may chose to write about the physical sensations, how you felt emotionally, or grains of spiritual wisdom that came to you when being bathed in this beautiful energy called Light of the Eternal One. Regardless of your experience, even if you felt nothing at all, write about it. For even if you felt nothing at all, what will come through in your writing is your own longing to connect with the Divine.

You may even want to be creative and begin using this journal to record your experience through poetry. Below are two of my own short poems that may offer inspiration:

Love's Mystery

Blame no one

Not even yourself

For that is to assume

you know

Gain the courage

to open your fists

like pomegranates

exposing the redness of Love's mystery

Beloved

Be loved by the universe
by making the universe
your beloved

Whether or not you decide to include poetry as part of your journaling activity, write down your thoughts, inspirations, feelings, and insights. This will help ground your experience, and also maps out in words the beautiful changes in your consciousness that will occur during the forty-day cycle you have embarked upon.

Mindful Diet and Mindful Action

What you put into your body, and what you put into the world through your actions, invariably will have an impact on your spiritual journey. And though it is not required that you accompany the forty-day cycle with a fast, it is recommended that you be mindful of what you choose to put into your body during this time, since you are going through profound changes in your energy system. Similarly, how you act in the world should also be given special care during this forty-day period.

Each person knows what feels right to them, so there is no exclusionary rule about what to eat, or what to do. All that is requested is that you should be especially mindful with respect to both of these areas of your life during the initial forty days of receiving the basic treatment. I believe that inside of each of us is an intuitive barometer that tells us when we have gone into excess. This is a time to listen to that barometer.

If you feel that it is in your best interest to refrain from eating certain foods or engaging in sexual activity during this time, then listen to that feeling. As that may be what is right for you, and not necessarily what is right for somebody else. Some may feel the need to completely give up alcohol at this time, and for others it may still be okay to have an occasional glass of wine. For others, the care may be in not consuming sugar, caffeine, or other substances that chemically influence consciousness. Again, there is no hard-and-fast rule, since each of us is different and has our own knowledge of what works and does not work for our own energy system. Being mindful does not mean starving yourself, making yourself miserable, or engaging in any self-punishing activity. It only means to listen at a very deep level to whether or not what you put into your own body and what you put into the world through your actions is in the highest good.

During this forty-day period simply listen to yourself at a very deep level, and trust that you know what is best. Part of the wonder of a true spiritual journey is in reclaiming the power of choice, and knowing that you as an individual are guided in that choice by being forever connected with the inexhaustible presence of the Divine. Listen with love, and trust that you more than anyone else know the best choices you can make for yourself during this sacred time.

6

Sharing the Basic Treatment with Others

Once you have received the Light of the Eternal One empowerment, not only can you offer basic energy treatments to yourself, but you can share this extraordinary gift with others as well. Though during the first forty days you should keep the focus primarily on maintaining your own daily practice, that does not mean that you cannot also offer basic treatments to friends and family during this initial period and beyond.

Performing the basic treatment on others is as simple as it is when performing it on yourself. To start, you will want to find a suitable setting where you and the other person will not be disturbed. Then, you will want share what you know about Light of the Eternal One, including any personal experiences with the energy that you find relevant. Since the person receiving the treatment is likely to have never heard of this energy before, sharing your own impressions of the energy will be of utmost value. Answer any questions to the best of your ability, and if you don't know the answer to any question the other person has, simply reply honestly, that you don't know. Eventually, the energy will speak for itself. But, making the person as comfortable as possible before they receive their first treatment is an important initial step.

Once you are both ready to begin the treatment, make sure the person receiving is sitting upright in a chair. Stand behind them and gently place your hands over the top of their head. You do not need to apply pressure, but simply allow your hands to rest there. Then, simply intend that Light of the Eternal One flow through your hands into their head. You may, if you wish, also invite any angels, ascended masters, or other Divine beings to be part of this process. As the energy begins to flow, you may feel it come in through your crown chakra, a sacred energy wheel at the top of your head, and move down through your hands into the person being treated. Know that as this happens, you are also receiving a portion of the Divine energy, just as is the case with Reiki and other Divine energy-healing modalities. You may, if you are intuitively inclined, actually see the energy as well. Most people see it as a sparkling white light, almost like a waterfall, coming down from the heavens. But even if you don't see it, or even feel it, simply keep your hands over the person's head and intend that the energy flow.

At a certain point you may sense that this white light has filled up the person's skull and is traveling down their spine throughout their entire nervous system. Again, since not everyone who is empowered to flow Light of the Eternal One will experience this, do not worry if you are one of those people who doesn't feel it.

In my many years of working with energy and other energy healers, I have found that some of the best healers are people who feel nothing at all and who are capable of going into that place of absolute trust and surrender to the Divine. Similarly, I have also known some individuals who are very adept at sensing subtle energies who are not always of the highest integrity. What that means is that there is no real relationship between being spiritual and being psychic. So, if you are not psychically sensing anything, don't worry about it and just keep your hands in the proper position until the five-minute treatment is complete. The real litmus test of this energy is not whether you or the other person actually feels it as it is flowing. The true test is in how it impacts you immediately afterwards. If, after the treatment, both you and the person receiving feel a sense of calm and inner peace, then you know that the treatment was a success.

Once the treatment is complete, gently pull your hands away from the person's head and quietly whisper to them to *be still*. Do not ask them questions or do anything that may break the moment of calm and peace that they most likely are now experiencing. If, at a later time, the person wants to share their experience of the energy, it is fine for them to do so. But, do not coerce or prod them into doing so, especially in those precious moments right after the treatment. Generally, if it is appropriate, I will walk away from the person and give them plenty of time to be alone with their experience, perhaps not even seeing them for the rest of the day.

Trust your instinct and do what feels right, but always respect the fact that Light of the Eternal One is an energy that brings each of us into a place of oneness with the Divine. And since the person receiving the treatment will, in effect, be in a state of energetic communion, to interrupt them for the sake of asking questions about their experience is something you should strictly avoid. Simply know that in sharing this Divine light with another, you have brought more joy into the world, and focus not on the experience of the other person, but on the beautiful feeling you are likely to have had by sharing this sacred and transformational gift with another.

7

Sending Light of the Eternal One Distantly Across Time and Space

It is possible to send Light of the Eternal One to anyone who wishes to receive it, even if they are not physically present. To do this, simply hold your hands with your palms facing outward and intend that Light of the Eternal One flow to the intended person. Since this light is eternal and one with all creation, it is not bound by the limits of time and space. So, upon intending that it arrive to anyone who is your recipient, it will simply manifest there. It does not flow in a straight line, but simply appears wherever you intend it to go.

To perform a long-distance treatment, it is desirable first to have the free will consent of the person you are sending the energy to. This does not mean that the energy will not flow if you do not have the person's consent, but it is simply not a good habit to send energy to people without their consent or knowledge. To do so robs them of their choice to participate or not participate in the healing.

I mention this because I have known too many energy healers who believe that they have the right to simply blast anyone they wish, at any given time, with or without consent, with whatever energy-healing modality they happen to be trained in. Not only does this set up a dysfunctional pattern of trying to heal people who do not wish to be healed, but it is also an energetic invasion of privacy. That being said, I do think there are some rare instances, like when someone is in a coma and unable to offer consent, when it is okay to send the energy after doing some form of divination, such as using a pendulum to see if the person truly consents to the treatment or not. But only in those rare cases—and only when the divination says *yes*—should you send others energy of any kind without their verbal or written agreement.

First, ask for the consent of the person you are going to be sending energy to. Once that consent is given, agree upon a mutually desirable time for the treatment to occur. To send the treatment, you simply place your hands so that your palms face away from you. Then, intend Light of the Eternal One to flow from your hands and arrive to the desired recipient. Do this for five minutes, or until you feel as if their skull and spinal cord have filled with the light. Since it may be harder to detect this at distance, simply sending a treatment for the five-minute time period is easier than trying to guess if the person you are sending to has filled up with the light.

Another way to do a long-distance treatment is to send it forward in time with the intention that it arrive when the person is next sleeping. Since this light is eternal, it is not bound by time in any way or form. The advantage in doing this form of treatment is that it gives you more freedom as to when to send a treatment, and does not bind you into sending it only at specific times. Since I often have standing agreements with other energy healers where we have given mutual consent to send treatments to each other at any time, using this technique in those situations is helpful. This way it does not interfere with any task the recipient of the treatment may be engaged in—such as driving a car on a busy freeway—at the time the treatment is originally being sent.

To send a treatment forward in time to when a person is sleeping, simply hold that intention while sending the energy. Otherwise, the process is exactly the same in that you place your hands with your palms facing away from you, and then intend Light of the Eternal One to flow to the desired person for five minutes. Again, add the intention in this scenario that it arrive forward in time, the next time the person is sleeping.

You can also use this same technique to send Light of the Eternal One to yourself, either backwards or forward in time. Again, the only difference would be in holding a specific intention about where the treatment should go with respect to time. The advantage of sending yourself treatments backwards in time is that you can immerse yourself with this light during difficult periods of your life, or when specific traumas occurred. Treating yourself at such points in time is desirable, for it coats any wounding that occurred at those points in your life with a loving light that, in effect, is the presence of the Divine. Try this on yourself and see the effect it has.

First, think of a time in your life when you experienced some kind of trauma, either physically, emotionally, or spiritually. Then, place your hands with your palms facing away from you and simply intend that Light of the Eternal One is flowing to you at that specific point in time. Hold this intention for at least five minutes, or longer if the trauma was severe. You may feel the odd sensation of the energy arriving to you backwards in time, which can shift your memory of the traumatic event. And, you may notice that any negative charge once associated with the event may begin to dissipate. Again, much will depend on the severity of the trauma. The most severe traumas may require numerous treatments before being fully released. But, now you have the ability to send energy treatments repeatedly to these painful points in the timeline of your life until they are fully healed.

Sending treatments forward in time works the same way, except instead of healing traumas that have yet to occur, you may be preventing new ones, or better yet, simply blessing yourself forward in time with the euphoric sensation that often occurs when being treated with Light of the Eternal One. Pick a time in the not-too-distant future when you think would be a good time to receive a treatment. This time can even be only minutes or hours into the future if you are eager to test this process. Once you have decided upon a specific time, simply place your hands so that your palms are facing away from you. Then, allow Light of the Eternal One to flow to you forward in time simply by holding that intention as the energy flows. Do this for five minutes, and then relax.

When the appointed time arrives for you to receive the treatment you have sent to yourself, make sure you find a comfortable place to sit or lie down so that you can fully enjoy the treatment and its effects. Note how you feel when receiving this treatment you have sent to yourself through time. You may want to write about this sensation in your journal, and specify any changes that happened for you after receiving the treatment. These changes can be emotional shifts, or shifts in consciousness as you expand your concept of time to be more fluid and in keeping with the quantum nature of this universe, in which time is but an illusion.

8

Opening the Path of Love

Light of the Eternal One has many functions. The basic treatment focuses on expanding your consciousness to see how inseparable and one with the Divine you truly are. That shift in consciousness can only deepen your spiritual path, allowing you to live lighter by knowing the depth of your connection to the Divine. Also, it can release old wounds and traumas on the physical, emotional, and spiritual level by shifting any trauma consciousness back into a place of oneness with the Divine. There are other treatments, however, besides the basic one.

The first of these treatments is one I refer to as *opening the path to love*. The purpose of this treatment is self-explanatory, in that it opens you deeper into a place of compassion and love. It does this by bringing Light of the Eternal One directly into the heart center, from which it then flows through the entire emotional body. Just as the basic treatment is simple and easy to learn, so too is this one.

Opening the path to love simply involves placing your hands on your heart instead of your head when giving yourself Light of the Eternal One. When I do this for myself, I tend to feel an expanded sense of compassion for all things, as well as a deeper sense of self-love that includes knowing the infinite love that the Divine has for me and all beings.

Try this treatment on yourself by simply placing your hands over your heart and intending Light of the Eternal One to flow into your heart through your hands. Hold this for at least five minutes, or until you feel that your heart is entirely filled with this light. You may want to journal on how this feels compared to how it feels to run the basic treatment on yourself.

My own sense is that the basic treatment works primarily on consciousness and awareness, whereas this treatment works primarily on the emotional body. When I first began teaching Light of the Eternal One to others, I noticed that some people felt drawn to place their hands on their head and others felt the call to place their hands over their heart. My sense is that each person intuitively knew what they needed and placed their hands in the appropriate location.

You can also combine the two treatments by placing one hand on the head and the other on the heart. However, my experience with this combined treatment is that some people really loved it and others found it a bit overwhelming. Those who found it overwhelming preferred to work on the head and heart separately. I do not think there is a right or wrong way of doing this, so experiment with these techniques and see what works for you. As long as you eventually work on both the head and the heart, it does not matter if you work on them separately or together.

When working on others, you can now either place your hands on their head, as in the basic treatment, or place your hands on the person's heart. I recommend, however, that for anyone experiencing Light of the Eternal One for the first time you should always use the basic treatment, with your hands on top of the person's head. This is because the basic treatment establishes that fundamental connection of deepening the person's relationship to the Divine, which is the primary purpose and foundation of all Light of the Eternal One treatments. Yet, in cases where the person has already experienced Light of the Eternal One, either option is fine to use, or you can use the combined treatment option of one hand on their head and the other over their heart. If using the combined option, however, ask the person beforehand to inform you if the treatment begins to feel overwhelming for them. If during the treatment they do indicate any sense of being overwhelmed, simply place both hands on either the head or heart—whichever one you feel intuitively drawn to work on during the treatment.

9

The Whole World in Your Hands

I remember that spiritual song "He's Got The Whole World In His Hands" when I think of the Light of Eternal One technique for working on specific issues and situations. The reason I think of this song is that it reminds me that we are always constantly being held by the love of the Divine. And for me, Light of the Eternal One is a primary example of how preciously each of us is held in Divine love. The technique that follows is one in which you will have the opportunity to hold the whole world—all your relationships and issues—in your own hands for the purpose of calling forth Light of the Eternal One into those relationships, issues, and situations and heal them.

The wonderful thing about Light of the Eternal One is that you can use it to accentuate that sense of Divine presence to emanate more into any particular situation or issue. To do this, first pick a life situation or life issue that you want to work on. Then, simply hold your hands together, with your pinkies touching and palms facing upward to the sky, as if you are about to hold a feather lightly in your hands. Now, intend that whatever situation or life issue you want to work on is being held in your hands, and then flow Light of Eternal One through your hands into that issue.

You may feel the presence of the Divine emanate stronger into that situation or issue the longer you flow Light of Eternal One. As with the basic treatment, you probably will not need to flow the energy for more than five minutes at any one given time, as you will feel a sense that the issue or situation has become filled with Light of the Eternal One. This does not mean the issue is now entirely healed, but simply that you have flowed enough energy into it for this one treatment. Know that treatments can be repeated over a period of time to deepen the long-term effects.

One treatment I recommend is to work on your relationship with your parents using this technique. It does not matter if your parents are living or dead, if you were close to them or not, or what degree of healing may need to occur there. For some who had good childhood experiences, you may feel that such a treatment is unnecessary. And for those who had extremely difficult childhood experiences with their parents, it may feel like: Why bother? Too much damage has been done to heal the situation. However, in working with this technique in my own life, I can only say that the promise it holds not only for healing, but also expanding your consciousness, is amazing.

My own experience with this technique has been that it has allowed me to see the inherent good in my parents, even the underlying essence of the

Divine that came through my parents to call me forth into this universe. Remember, Light of the Eternal One is not just a healing modality, but something more. It calls forth that very Divine presence that sustains the universe. When you think of the line from Genesis where God says *Let there be light*, it is that light I am referring to when writing about Light of the Eternal One. And to call that light through your relationship with your parents, regardless of what your experience of them has been in this life, is a mind-altering Divine ride into the beauty of how amazing the very concept of bearing children is, when seen from a Divine perspective. With that in mind, now begin the work of performing this technique to send Light of the Eternal One into your relationship with your parents.

I recommend doing this technique one parental relationship at a time. Know that in performing this technique you are not sending Light of the Eternal One to either of your parents, but are emanating it into the energetic cords, memories, and karmic debris that exists *between* you and that parent. So, with this technique it is not necessary to ask for their consent, since they are not receiving a Light of the Eternal One treatment.

For the purpose of relating to the source of your birth, I recommend performing this technique first on your relationship with your mother. Again, the potential for healing is deep, regardless of the essence of that relationship.

Begin the treatment by bringing your hands together, touching at the pinkies with palms facing up toward the sky, almost as if you are begging for food. Now, imagine that in your hands you are holding that relationship with your mother, as if that relationship is a feather that has delicately landed on both palms. If you wish to visualize a shape or color for the relationship, you can do that. But all that is necessary is simply holding the intent that your relationship with your mother is being held in your hands.

Now, intend that Light of the Eternal One flow through your hands into that relationship. Again, it does not matter if your mother is dead or alive, living near or far, for this technique to work. As you hold your hands there, emanating Light of the Eternal One into that relationship, you may feel any old wounds rise to the surface for a healing. Yet, underneath any old wounds you will bridge that Divine presence deeper into the lineage of who you are in this life. And it is this bridging effect that is the most important aspect of this treatment.

The healing of any old wounds will seem almost like a by-product compared to this bridging effect of deepening to your own lineage, your own path of light that brought you into existence and was always underscored with a Divine presence. Believe me, as one who had a horrible childhood—one filled with emotional, sexual, and physical abuse—I know the temptation to disregard this concept at its core. And yet I can only say that the first time I performed this technique, I had a deep appreciation for the eternal aspect of my mother that is beyond her personality in this life, beyond any abuse she caused upon me.

And in seeing and relating to that light, I could see and relate to her spirit on an entirely new level. This does not mean it erases my past with her, but it does mean that now I can decide which level of reality I want to know this relationship from: the one bogged-down in the wounds of personality, or the one of Divine light that brought me into this world.

My words may not do justice to this technique, and so I can only encourage you to try it yourself. Hold the intention for at least five minutes, or until the space above your hands feels like it is filled with Light of the Eternal One. Then, let your hands rest and give thanks to the Divine in whatever name works best for you for the opportunity of this transformational healing.

After having performed this technique on your relationship with your mother, do the same technique on your relationship with your father. Again, bring your hands together, pinkies touching and palms facing up. Imagine that in your hands you are holding the relationship between you and your father, regardless of how close or distant that relationship may be or may have been. Now, simply intend that Light of the Eternal One is flowing through your hands into that relationship. Feel any old wounds come to the surface for a healing as you hold your intention that this light keep flowing for approximately five minutes. As you do this, you will be creating a Divine bridge of light into the lineage you have with your father. That light is healing, loving, and will release many of the wounds that may have occurred between you and your father in this life, regardless of how good or how challenging a father he may actually have been.

You may feel after approximately five minutes that the space above your hands feels full of light. Even if you don't feel this, it is best to end the treatment after a five-minute period of time so that the impact of the treatment does not overwhelm you. Know that you can always revisit this technique for working further on this relationship, your relationship with your mother, or any other relationship. Now, gently allow your hands to rest and give thanks to the Divine for this wonderful and transformational healing.

Use this technique on your relationship with other significant people in your life as well, be they siblings, friends, significant others, mentors, or teachers. I especially recommend using it in relationships where there is difficulty. The power of this technique will shed light on how best to navigate through any troubled aspects of those relationships. And it will bridge that relationship deeper into its Divine core, impacting how you communicate and act on all levels with respect to the other party, or parties, involved.

Know that in using this technique you are drawing that sacred light that sustains all creation deeper into those relationships, those areas of your life that are most important to you. You are literally taking your life into your hands, and emanating into your life that Divine essence that is at the core of all things.

10

Lighting the Way
of Your Life Path

Light of the Eternal One can assist you in all of your relationships, including your relationship with your life path, or life purpose. You can focus this light on that aspect of your life by using the same technique outlined in the previous chapter. The only difference is that instead of intending the light to work on a relationship with another person, you intend that it work on your relationship to your life path.

Try this now by bringing your hands together, touching at the pinkies, with your palms facing up to the sky. Imagine that in your hands you are holding your life path. If you want to visualize that path as an object or color, feel free to do so, but all that truly matters is that you have the intention that your life path is now being held in your own hands. Now, flow Light of the Eternal One through your hands into your life path. As you do this, you may feel strong sensations about whether or not you are going down the right path in life, or if there are any major obstacles on your path coming up in the near future. Keep holding your intention as the energy flows and remember that a five-minute treatment can create a large shift for most people. To be able to handle ongoing treatments and not be overwhelmed, it is suggested that you not go more than five minutes during any one treatment, and that you not do more than one treatment per day on this particular issue. When the five minutes is up, give thanks to the Divine and let your hands rest.

You may want to journal about any insights about your life's path that you had during the treatment. Remember, journaling helps ground the treatment. And it also helps you capture those sometimes fleeting images and messages that are all too important to let slip away. Write them down, even if they seem insignificant. You may be surprised how often those messages that seem insignificant can turn out to be the most important.

If you are someone who feels you are living your life with purpose, doing a regular treatment of this kind will simply allow you to fine-tune your life, and keep things flowing as they should with additional support of the Divine. And, if you are someone who feels unsure of what your life path is, then this treatment will be key to getting you on track. Just perform the treatment regularly, perhaps even making it part of your daily practice, until you begin to feel like you know your life purpose and are living it.

Bringing the Light Into Daily Life

The simple technique for bringing Light of the Eternal One into your relationships, including your relationship to your life path, can also be expanded to bring light into each aspect of daily living. Light of the Eternal One can be used to assist your life at work, in the home, and even to clear the energy of a room or workspace.

Let's begin with how Light of the Eternal One can be used to make your work life flow smoother, easier, and with less stress and fewer complications. The best time to do this would be before you arrive at work, so that the energy is already set for your day with no surprises when you arrive. Again, to do this you would use the technique described in the previous chapter, with your hands touching at the pinkies, palms facing up toward the sky. Then, imagine that your workday is resting in the palms of your hands, that you are holding your own experience of what the future of your workday will be. Begin flowing Light of the Eternal One through your hands into your workday. Do this for five minutes, or until the space above your hands feels filled with light.

As you perform the treatment, as with other Light of the Eternal One treatments, you may sense relevant issues rise to the surface to be healed. In other words, if you have an issue with a coworker, you may sense that issue rise up to the surface and then feel the energy become more calm and smooth as Light of the Eternal One assists in bringing that issue back into a place of oneness with the Divine to help create the best of all possible outcomes between you and your coworker with regard to that issue.

This is just one example of how Light of the Eternal One can improve your work life on a daily basis. Even if the issue is not with a coworker, and is more about reaching a deadline, or having a smoother flow of clients that makes you day less stressful, Light of the Eternal One works on all of these possibilities by accentuating into your workday the underlying Divine light that is the basis of creation.

Similarly, this same process can be used in the home. If you are a parent who is struggling to cook dinner for the kids, clean the house, or get things done around the home, the process used for bringing Light of the Eternal One into your life at home is the same as for bringing that light into your work life each day.

A good routine is when you get up in the morning, after performing the basic treatment on yourself, perform a treatment to make your day flow easier at home. Again, do this by holding your hands together, touching at the pinkies with palms facing up toward the sky. Then imagine your day at home is like a gentle flower that is being held in your hands. Now, intend that Light of the Eternal One flow through your hands into the flower—and therefore into your home life— for the rest of the day. While you are performing this treatment, you may feel issues arise that are relevant to your home life. Simply know this is Light of the Eternal One bringing that issue to the surface for a healing. Hold the intention that the energy flow for five minutes, or until the space above you hands feels filled with light. If you feel no issues arise at all, take that as a good sign and that there is probably little that needs to be resolved with respect to your day at home. Know that in such situations where no issues arise, Light of the Eternal One is still working for the highest good by simply blessing your day.

You can also use Light of the Eternal One in other easy ways as part of your daily life. Just as you can send this wonderful energy into your day at work or at home, you can also fill a room or other space with this joyous light to help create a better ambience: An ambience that effectively promotes the highest good and fills the space with a deeper sense of Divine presence.

To perform the treatment for a room, simply cup your hands together like you have captured a butterfly. Imagine that inside of cupped space between your hands is the room or space you want to fill with Light of the Eternal One. Then, just flow the energy through your hands until the cupped space between your hands feels entirely filled with light, or for approximately five minutes. Depending on the size of the actual room, know there are some very large spaces that may take longer than the usual five minutes to fill the space with Light of the Eternal One. Trust your intuition in those cases to let you know when the treatment is complete.

If you happen to be present in the room you are working on, you will notice the energy shift to a more beautiful vibration as you perform the treatment, a vibration filled with harmony and joy. If you are not present in that room when you are treating it—as might be the case when sending a treatment to your workspace from home—know that when you arrive you will be greeted with an ambience that is sweet and that coats everything with the presence of Divine love. This effect can only enhance all that you do, and add to the ongoing deepening of your spiritual path by bringing that Divine presence into those spaces where you live and work. Once you have performed a treatment on a room, it will usually last for the entire day, depending on what other energies might be impacting the space. Repeated treatments over time simply deepen the effect, like adding extra coats of paint to a wall to enhance a particular color for a room. As with the other treatments mentioned in this chapter, this one can add to creating a more joyous life on a daily basis, by bringing that Divine presence into the places where you work and live.

12

Honoring Your Body

Light of the Eternal One is primarily an energy that is focused to shift our consciousness—or the consciousness in any given issue, relationship, or situation—back into a place of oneness with the Divine. Still, that does not mean that it has no value with respect to physical healing or supporting the physical body. Remember, many forms of disease are an expression of emotional and spiritual imbalance. So, to offer Light of the Eternal One treatments on your physical body will help sustain a measure of good health.

When you are performing the basic treatment, with your hand on your head, you are getting some physical benefit to the treatment. For as you deepen into your relationship with the Divine, that will also naturally translate into a betterment of your physical condition. However, you can accentuate the physical healing aspect of any treatment simply by intending physical healing while the energy is flowing through your hands. In other words, you can perform a basic treatment and simply hold the intention that it be directed primarily to your physical body.

During such a treatment, you simply hold your hands on top of your head as has been shown for the basic treatment. But, intend that Light of the Eternal One flow directly into all the cells of your body, to nourish your body and support it in whatever way is necessary at this point in time. This way the energy is flowing through all of you, not just your brain and nervous system as happens in the basic treatment. Hold the intention and keep your hands on top of your head for approximately five minutes. After the five-minute period, let your hands down from your head and rest. Also, give thanks to the Divine for the blessing of the treatment you just received.

In cases where there is a specific illness, injury, or disease that needs to be addressed, you can adjust the above treatment accordingly. Simply place your hands over or near the area of your body most directly impacted by the physical ailment. Hold your hands there for more than five minutes if the ailment is severe. Since the energy is working more at a cellular level, and not as much on your consciousness, you are less likely to experience any sensations of being overwhelmed if the treatment goes for a prolonged period of time. In these instances, simply let the energy run for as long as feels appropriate. And when the treatment ends, give thanks to the Divine as you would after any Light of the Eternal One treatment.

Maintain a regular practice of honoring the physical body with Light of the Eternal One. When I perform such treatments on myself, it feels almost like the cells of my body are singing, and I imagine them each as individual angels singing the names of God the way angels are said to do in heaven. I know this light sustains my physical being, and can fine-tune each cell in my body to function at the highest level. Know as well that if you feel ill or in need of special care, the energy that sustains the universe is now available to you through your own hands. Take charge of your own healing process by using Light of the Eternal One to your supreme physical benefit, both as a daily, energetic tonic for the entire body and to support those areas of the body in need of more direct healing.

13

Food as a Path to the Divine

Eating is one of the great pleasures in life, and previously in this book I mentioned the importance of eating mindfully, of bringing into your body those foods that are for your highest good. Also, in the previous chapter, the emphasis was on honoring your body. One specific way of using Light of the Eternal One for both enhancing the joy of eating and honoring your body at a deeper level is to perform a Light of the Eternal One treatment on your food.

This concept of pouring Divine energy into food is not new, and is something generally taught in Reiki and other Divine energy healing forms. There are several ways this can be done with Light of the Eternal One. The easiest is simply to place your hands a few inches above your plate before you eat, and allow Light of the Eternal One to flow from your hands into the food that is just a few inches away. Remember, it is not necessary for your hands to be touching the food any more than your hands would need to touch the physical body of someone to whom you would be sending energy in a long-distance treatment. Just hover your hands over the plate a few inches away and intend that Light of the Eternal One flow from your hands into your food.

Another way you can also empower your food with a Light of the Eternal One treatment is to view an entire meal as a situation, and then use the treatment process for situations and relationships. To do this, simply place your hands side by side, pinkies touching with your palms facing upward. Imagine the entire meal, including any beverages, side dishes, or desserts, being held in miniature form in the palms of your hands, almost as if your hands were the table upon which the meal is being served. Then, flow Light of the Eternal One from your hands, envisioning it going into the meal as a whole, bathing each molecule of food with this joyous light.

If you want to add even more energy to this process, you can also flow Light of the Eternal One into the preparation and cooking of the meal. Again, just treat that as an entire situation—just as you would work or a relationship—bringing your hands together side by side, and imagining you are holding the very process of the meal's creation in your hands, while intending that Light of the Eternal One flow into this entire process. For some people that may seem a bit too extravagant just for a meal, but if you have ever eaten a meal that has been spiritually blessed (something that is a key draw for those who enjoy food prepared at Hare Krishna temples), then you will want to add this additional touch to your enjoyment of food.

Remember that in honoring the food and blessing the process of how it is prepared, you are also eventually ingesting that blessing into your own body. In other words, it is in keeping with the clichéd but true saying: You are what you eat. And if you continuously bless the food that is eventually to become part of yourself, then you are essentially blessing yourself; blessing each future cell of your being. This will strengthen the health of your body, as well as shift your consciousness each time you consume a meal that has been blessed with Light of the Eternal One energy. Try this on your own food for a week and see if you notice a difference in how you feel mentally, emotionally, and how your body feels physically. Over time, this routine can be a major aspect of the deepening of your spiritual practice, as well as maintaining optimum physical health.

14

Clearing the Karmic Body

Karma is like accumulated energetic residue of our actions, both good and bad. Also, as we progress from one life to the next, that residue and debris remains with us from previous lifetimes. As we create more and more of that residue and debris, it can draw us to situations that can either help us resolve a karmic issue, or slide deeper into it, like quicksand. Clearing the karmic body is sort of like an energetic housecleaning of that body. It isn't that you can rid yourself of every speck of karmic dust, but you can clean things up enough so that life feels better and you can move more easily, with freedom of choice to where you want to really go on your soul journey.

Light of the Eternal One can help in clearing out much of the karmic residue and debris from previous actions, both from this life and other lifetimes.

To run Light of the Eternal One into the karmic body, simply treat the karmic body the same way you would a situation or relationship, by placing your hands side by side, pinkies touching and palms facing up to the sky. Then, imagine that your karmic body is a light feather, resting over both of your palms. Now, intend that Light of the Eternal One flow though your hands into your karmic body. As you do this, you may feel some energy move and shift in the area of your spine, which is often where a great deal of our karmic baggage is stored. Keep running the energy as you feel the space above your hands, and probably the space around your spinal column, fill with Light of the Eternal One. As with other treatments, I recommend keeping it to only five minutes, simply because you will need time to integrate any clearing that has occurred, and if you try to clear too much karmic debris and residue from your karmic body at once, it can be overwhelming for some people.

Please know that you will never achieve an entirely clear karmic body. As long as you exist in physical form, you are going to have some karma to work out. If you didn't, you would not be on this plane of existence. However, clearing the karmic body as a regular practice can assist you in feeling more freedom in your life.

The way karma can influence your life choices is like this: Imagine that karmic debris and residue are like asteroids that have merged together to form a planet. As this imaginary planet grows in size, it begins to create gravity that can pull other objects toward it. This is similar to how karma works. If you have a huge clump of karmic debris or residue around an issue of feeling unworthy, this is creating a kind of gravitational field that will call in more and more situations for you to feel unworthy. Then, it becomes difficult to simply snap out of it and move on to a place of good self-esteem.

This is why so often conventional therapy can fail: When the person in therapy knows the behavior patterns they want to change, and the psychological reasons for those behavior patterns, but they simply cannot change them, no matter how hard they try. Often, this is because there is a karmic obstacle that conventional therapy is not prone to acknowledge or deal with.

If you are aware of a particular karmic issue when performing a treatment on your karmic body, you can intend that Light of the Eternal One flow directly into the karmic issue to help clear it out. Otherwise, general clearing of the karmic body on a regular weekly basis is recommend to both lighten your spiritual load, allow you to feel more freedom in life, and step deeper toward a relationship of oneness with the Divine.

15

Piercing the Veil of Maya

Maya is the great illusion. It is what keeps us imagining that we are alone in the universe, that we are separate from God. Sometimes, when having mystical experiences, the vision of some poets, mystics, artists, and others engaged in the exploration of human consciousness has pierced through this veil and eternity is grasped, the ego deflates, and one knows that there is no real struggle, no real dramas to be played out, but that all is just the never-ending love and presence of the Divine. Such experiences are referred to in some Buddhist texts, in the poetry of Rumi, and in the artwork of modern-day visionary artists such as Alex Grey. We do have the capacity to see through this veil, but unfortunately that seeing is often temporary, and then we fall back into the dream of being alone and separate in the universe, apart from God, Goddess, the Divine Creator of all that is.

In my own spiritual journey I have had experiences like the ones mentioned above, where the illusion falls away temporarily, though sometimes for longer periods of time than what one normally might think. Sometimes for me this seeing through the veil would last for weeks at a time, but eventually it would return to the place of illusion, and again I would fall into the dream of being separate from the Divine.

Over the past few years, however, I have begun to hear wonderful stories of people energetically releasing the veil, or aspects of it, on a permanent basis through energy work such as Reiki, Rei Ju, and other forms of Divine energy healing. Though the terminology in the various forms of energy healing may differ, eventually the true goal of awakening seems to be the same.

My work with permanently piercing my own veil involved a number of energy modalities, including advanced Reiki techniques that involve the higher self, a new form of energy work I call Magical Awakening, and Light of the Eternal One. The veil of Maya that exists within my own energy system now is pierced enough so that if I choose, I can go into that space of knowing my connection to the Divine at will, that place of knowing that we are one. This does not mean that I have lost all of my spiritual baggage, that I never get upset or lead a perfectly flawless life. For that picture of spiritual awakening is part of the greater illusion of Maya, and is one which, from what I can tell, does not even exist. But what does exist is the opportunity for all to return to a place of knowing their place of oneness with the Divine if they so chose to work on piercing the veil of Maya.

My sense is that any of the energy forms I used to pierce the veil of Maya within my own energy system is sufficient on its own to do the job, though some energy forms may work faster than others. But since this book is about Light of the Eternal One, I will keep the focus on how you can use this mode of energy healing to work on piercing a permanent hole in the veil of Maya within your own energetic body.

To work on the veil of Maya using light of the Eternal One, you use the technique for situations and relationships. Place your hands side by side, pinkies touching with your palms facing upward. Then, imagine you are holding the veil of Maya in your hands. If you want to embellish this aspect with your imagination, you can do so by seeing this veil as a gray or black film, a curtain, a wall, or maybe even a blindfold. Use whatever imagery calls to you most effectively when thinking about this veil. Once you are ready, begin flowing Light of the Eternal One through your hands into the veil. Do this for approximately five minutes, or until you feel as if your veil has become filled with light. Then, let your hands rest by your side as you notice the sensation of having this veil filled with Divine light. You may want to journal about this experience, as it will probably feel different than any of the treatments you have done so far using Light of the Eternal One.

I confess that one treatment of this kind is not likely to pierce the veil. What happens, though, is that you are bathing your veil with Divine light. That Divine light, when bathing the veil repeatedly over time, will slowly begin to affect the Divine consciousness of which the veil is made. Remember, everything is made from the Divine and therefore carries within it a spark of Divine consciousness. When trying to pierce the veil, it is not so much that you are trying to destroy it or release it as much as you are trying to awaken parts of the veil into remembering that it is, in fact, Divine consciousness, albeit a Divine consciousness that has fallen into a dream state.

My own sensations when running Light of the Eternal One into my veil—which I still do even though it has been pierced—is a great sensation of emptiness and peace, often accompanied with a deep sense of joy. This is a profound feeling, but less of the spiritual high or complete euphoria I sometimes get when simply doing the basic treatment. My sense is that this happens because in going directly to the veil, I am reminded on a deeper level of my own illusionary presence, or the fact that no *I* really does exist. And therefore, even though there is great peace and deep joy in this feeling, it is not the kind of intense euphoria of this imaginary *I* believing it has united with the One, which unfortunately is part of the greater dream and not as real as this deep emptiness filled with a joyful, quiet peace.

If the explanation above is confusing, try not to think too much about it and simply perform the treatment on the veil of Maya repeatedly over a period of months and track your own experience. As this veil begins to slide back into a waking state, into knowing itself as Divine, a portion of it may open entirely into a permanent waking state. When that happens, it is no longer an aspect of the veil, but a clear porthole through which you can see. And that is when you will know you have pierced the veil: When that porthole is always there and you can shift your consciousness to view life from that porthole at your own will. It is like having a peephole into reality. Once that peephole is there, the illusion of being separate from the Divine may still creep up from time to time, but from that point forward you will always know it is an illusion and that you can escape that illusion by simply shifting your consciousness and choosing to look at life through that peephole: That place in your own consciousness where the veil is pierced.

The more you continue working on the veil using Light of the Eternal One, the more that piercing of the veil will widen, allowing more truth, more clear vision, to come into your consciousness. And with that comes more freedom, as you are less and less bound to living out the dream story of this imaginary *I*. Instead, you can bask in Divine presence, and know your life more as an effortless, eternal laugh than as a dramatic story that has a start and a finish.

Make working on the veil of Maya, that aspect of Divine consciousness that has fallen into a dream state and is part of your energy system, a regular practice. Whether you do it daily or weekly, make a dedicated practice of working to pierce the veil. In doing so, your entire life will change for the better, and you will be on your path toward awakening from lifetimes of illusion and embracing your Divine right of knowing your true place in heaven, as an inseparable part of the presence of God.

$$\left(16\right)$$

Engaging in Spiritual Service

I write this book not just for the benefit of those who will read it and use the techniques provided in these chapters, but also for the greater good of all beings. As humanity evolves and more and more people awaken to their true Divine nature, this wave of spiritual awakening will impact all that we do as a species. It will shift how we treat the planet, and how we interact with the fellow creatures we share this beautiful earth with. My hope is that it will create a better, more spiritually minded species that is further invested in the common good and in serving the Divine purpose than in just serving our own needs.

As part of the goal of seeing humanity as a whole evolve, and not just be concerned with our own spiritual awakening, I encourage creating all who become empowered with Light of the Eternal One to have a practice of selfless service to accompany the work you do on yourself energetically.

This may mean that you devote time each week to send Light of the Eternal One to issues around the planet where healing is needed, as in places where there is war, strife, genocide, or other such maladies that impact humankind. It is not that one person sending a treatment to these issues will rid the planet of them. But over time, as more and more people awaken not only to their own Divine nature, but also to their immense capacity for energetic healing, we together—the greater *We*—can begin to address some of our planetary concerns not simply by relying on political solutions, but also by sending waves of healing light to these situations. For I have seen how even one person sending energy to a small-scale situation can impact that situation for positive good. I imagine how much better a world we would have if on a weekly or even daily basis thousands of people were sending powerful forms of healing light, such as Light of the Eternal One, to bring peace in the Middle East, improve our relationship to the planet and its myriad other forms of life, or any other such worthy cause. If enough people did this, if the *We* was big enough, the world would change for the better.

It is with this vision in mind that I encourage you to meditate on what cause you would like to support through either an energetic contribution, financial contribution, or by offering time as a volunteer, to any cause of your choice that you believe helps create a better world. In some eastern traditions they would refer to this as *karma yoga*, as an act of selfless service to the greater good, without any thought or expectation that it will cause you personal gain.

I encourage this not simply from the sincere place of wanting to see a better world and knowing the impact the greater *We* can have when mobilized, but also because I know it will deepen your spiritual practice. For even though there are great strides that can be made in one's own spiritual evolution through the kind of energy work laid out in this book, if it is not tempered with some kind of spiritual service it is easy for one to slip into a place of spiritual narcissism.

I mention this not just from a place of theory, but because I have seen it. And at times I have been guilty as a teacher of placing too much emphasis on the energy work and not enough emphasis on the practices of giving, being kind, and loving each other as we should love ourselves. I have seen the results of such a path where it is all energy work and no humility, no work for the betterment of others. And, that unfortunately can result in creating a kind of self-obsessed person who has the appetite of an energy junkie, always in search for the next spiritual high, who does little, if anything, to lift the overall vibration of their community or the world.

It is even possible in cases such as these that the person can still pierce the veil of Maya, using their extraordinary energetic skills. But, if they have not worked on tempering the ego by selflessly serving the greater good, the overall gains of such spiritual energy work can be inconsequential. What you have, then, is still a self-interested person, but one with expanded consciousness: Someone who can see the veil of Maya is an illusory dream, but who then uses that dream state to simply indulge themselves. I have also seen some who turn the piercing of the veil into a kind of competition, as if they are somehow higher on the spiritual plane for having discovered that they themselves are part of the Divine. Unfortunately, these same souls often forget that everyone else is part of this same Divine being. And without that insight, even with the clear vision of knowing your own Divine presence, you lose sight of the true meaning of spirituality, which is always love.

Therefore, to bring love into your practice of energy work, by using that work to serve others and serve the highest good, you are engaging in the kind of spiritual service that is truly necessary to grow humility, sincere kindness, and an egoless love of your fellow beings on this earth, both human and nonhuman. And there is no form of energy work or energy treatment that I know of that can replace this form of selfless service. It is an essential ingredient in the recipe of spiritual growth.

I encourage you to find a path of selfless service that suits you. It may involve sending energy to great causes, as mentioned in the early paragraphs of this chapter. Or it may be as simple as volunteering time at a nursing home, or teaching illiterate people how to read, or helping out at a soup kitchen. The path this book offers is powerful and life-changing, but unless that is tempered with some type of karma yoga, some way of giving to the overall betterment of the planet without expecting a reward in return, then you risk falling into that abyss of those who see themselves as enlightened, but who do little for the creation of a better world, who essentially have overstepped their connection to the greater We that is working to liberate the Divine in us all.

17

Restoring the Garden of Eden

The Garden of Eden may have been real, or may just be a metaphor for that time and place before humanity fell into the illusion of existing in separation from the Divine. Either way, with Light of the Eternal One, it is possible to restore that sense of innocent connection to all things around you. You may have noticed this while working with the situational and relationship treatments mentioned earlier in this book. But it is possible to intend a more expanded version of the situational and relationship treatments to widen the circle of what we consider family, and what we think of as being in important relationship to us.

Start this by simply intending to do a relationship treatment between you and all the life forms that exist in your neighborhood, including any plants or animals. How big you decide to draw that circle that you may call the boundary of your neighborhood is up to you, but begin so that it is large enough to challenge you, but not so large as to overwhelm you. Then, having decided what area constitutes your neighborhood, prepare your hands for the treatment by touching them side by side at the pinkies, with palms facing upward. Now, imagine *your relationship* to all these life forms in your neighborhood existing like a feather in the palm of your hands and begin flowing Light of the Eternal One into your connection to all of these beings. This process should include any animals, plants, and people you don't know well or have never met. Again, you are not flowing Light of the Eternal One to them, but into your relationship with them.

Continue the treatment for five minutes, or until you feel that the space above your hands is entirely filled with light. Then, let the treatment come to a close by allowing your hands to come back down, resting them in your lap or at your side.

This is where the interesting part begins. And you may want to journal about it. Notice how you feel now about each tree, each plant, each animal in your neighborhood. Do they now seem more like they are a part of you, one with you in a way you cannot describe? Do you now feel more friendly toward people in your neighborhood who you never knew? Again, write about these feelings.

In my own experience with this treatment, I first began using it while on the island of Bali. And I would perform the treatment first on my relationship to all the Balinese on the island, whether or not I knew them personally. I would do this as one short treatment, lasting five minutes or less. What I felt in these treatments was a deeper sense of compassion for each Balinese person, whether I knew them or not. I also felt less like an alien to their culture, even though I speak only a slight amount of Indonesian, the official language in Bali. I love Bali and had been to it many times, but now I felt a much deeper connection to the people of this land in a way I had not minutes prior, before I had performed the treatment.

Later, I began expanding this technique to include the rice fields, palm trees, and many flowering plants that are part of this island's beautiful habitat. And, as with the previous treatment, I suddenly felt a deeper sense of connection to the island itself, and all the life that lived upon it.

Try this treatment for a week, just using your neighborhood as the primary focus. Perform the treatment each day, and journal about your feelings and sensations afterwards. See what changes may come from a committed practice of doing this for just one week. You may suddenly find you have new friends, or at least a friendlier way of looking at those you share your neighborhood with. After trying this on your neighborhood for one week, try it on a larger circle of what you wish to call your community, maybe an entire town or city area. Again, journal about your experience after each treatment. As you continue working with this, you may feel the energy simply soften between you and the community you live in, as if any sense of alienation between you and that community is dissolving. Try this for one week, and see how it changes your life in that community.

You can, of course, continue expanding that circle each week, until it is as large as you wish for it to be. But refrain from making it too large in the beginning, or you may feel overwhelmed by the results. Go at your own pace, and as you do this it will slowly restore that sense of innocence and wonder you once probably had about the world. You can keep extending that circle until it engulfs the entire planet, and then with regular treatments at this level you begin to know the greater We of which we are all part.

This technique works best when starting with a sense of geography, but you can also shift the intention of it to work on larger communities that are not bound by geographic boundaries. You may want to work on any issues you have with those of the opposite sex, or those of the same sex, by simply doing a treatment on your relationship to all the men or all the women of the world. Again, it is not that you are flowing Light of the Eternal One to all of these people, but you are working on your relationship to each gender by performing such treatments.

As a man, often we are taught a sense of distrust of intimacy with fellow men. Yet when performing this treatment on my relationship with men in general, I feel a sense of lightening of that distrust, a sense of seeing other men as my spiritual brothers as opposed to being competitors. And similarly, when I perform this treatment on my relationship to women—to all women—I sense a deep appreciation of women, an intuitive understanding of our differences, as well as an appreciation of those differences. This treatment can also help individuals recovering from sexual abuse learn to regain trust of whichever gender they perhaps have grown suspicious of, owing to their abuse.

What I find amazing with this work is the potential to heal not only gender issues, but also racial, religious, and other barriers we create. For underneath all of these supposed differences, we all come from the same Creator, the same One. And by repeatedly using this technique, you can slowly begin to restore your own personal sense of the Garden of Eden, at least in the metaphorical sense of seeing the wholeness that is there in all things, as opposed to the differences. Use this process in your own work of healing the separation consciousness that affects us all. And as more and more people begin to do this work, we will begin to know the greater We, the We that is interconnected beyond all boundaries and is the guiding spirit in the next step of human evolution.

18

Light of the Eternal One and Your Higher Self

Those who have read two of my other books *The Reiki Magic Guide To Self-Attunement* (Crossing Press, 2007) and *Reiki For Spiritual Healing* (Crossing Press, 2009) know that much of my work involves learning techniques for connecting with the higher self, and using that connection to deepen the process of spiritual growth. In Reiki, this process has allowed many new and innovative processes to be discovered for how to use Reiki, ways that were not previously possible before these higher-self techniques were revealed. And, the same is true for Light of the Eternal One in that there are many more options for you to use once your higher self is empowered with this energy and you learn how to access Light of the Eternal One at that level. But first, it is important to mend your relationship with your higher self, a relationship many people do not even know exists.

Many cultures reference the concept of a higher self, but most of my experience is with reference to ancient Egyptian esoteric concepts and those concepts from the Hawaiian shamanic path of Huna. In both of these worldviews there is the idea of an energetic body, or mode of consciousness, that exists for us beyond this physical incarnation that in some ways is like a Divine parent and yet simultaneously part of who we are. This aspect of ourselves is waiting to be discovered so it can assist us on our soul journey.

In Huna, the primary role of this body is to promote healing, which it can do through garnering energy from the subconscious or conscious mind in order to perform the healing request made of the higher self. Often, this is done by rubbing the hands together to create *mana*, or energy. Mana can also be created through offering breath to the higher self. Once the higher self has the sufficient energy to perform the task at hand, it will, as long as that task is for the highest good.

Ancient Egyptians had a similar view of the higher self, which they saw as an energetic aspect of the human being that was almost Godlike, called the *Sahu*. This energetic body existed beyond this physical realm of time and space, and could be accessed through both breath and the proper use of words and intention. Using this Sahu to bring one's own energetic field into proper alignment was at the core of much ancient Egyptian esoteric writing.

It is important with this work to realize that there is a subtle difference between your higher self and that Divine presence you seek to be one with by piercing the veil of Maya. They are not the same. The Divine is, essentially, God or Goddess or the

Creator, known by many Divine names. Your higher self is not that, though it can be in a closer range of communication with the Divine realm, and therefore is wiser and sees with a clearer spiritual vision than you, here in body, are capable of. The higher self also has access to all your lifetimes, all actions that you are part of through all time and space. But, unlike the Divine, the higher self is not the ultimate Creator, although it, like everything, is itself made of Divine consciousness. The higher self is simply an energetic aspect of you that is in closest proximity to being Divine.

This, obviously, creates a kind of paradox to say that we are all one, but that our higher self isn't the same as the Divine. It both is and isn't, in the same way that each of us is both created from the Divine, and therefore carry in us an aspect of that Divine being. And yet, even when I am in that place of knowing my deep connection of oneness with the Divine, I still am not God, but simply *of God*. The same is true of the higher self, it is *of God*, but is not actually the Divine being from which all creation sprang forth.

All of this will be understood better once you begin working with your higher self energetically, as there are limits to how far language can reach in expressing concepts that are multidimensional and eternal, and that on some levels defy our basic understanding of the universe. In order to gain a better relationship with your own higher self, begin performing the relationship treatment on *your relationship to your own higher self* on a regular basis. To do this, place your hands side by side, pinkies touching and palms facing the sky. Then, imagine that you are holding your relationship with your higher self in your hands, or see that relationship as a feather lightly resting in your palms. Now, begin flowing Light of the Eternal One into that relationship.

As you do this, you may have the sensation of an aspect of yourself that is outside of your body, a presence that perhaps fills the room you are in, and yet is beyond this. Or, you may feel very little at all. Journal about your experience and see what insights may come to you while journaling.

Sometimes the act itself of wanting to initiate a real relationship with our higher self can be the start of real communication between you and your higher self, which can manifest through intuitive messages, messages from dreams, and other ways your higher self may choose to express itself to you. Journal. Write. Pay attention. Continue this treatment until your higher self begins to communicate to you. When that happens, entirely new doors of intuition and wisdom will open to you, which will expand the level of joy and self-knowledge in your life.

19

Freeing the Subconscious Mind

For many, the subconscious mind is the true key to spiritual awakening. For even though one can wish to attain high levels of spiritual expression, through acts of devotion and clearing energetic debris from our system, if the subconscious mind is still filled with fear or unresolved trauma, then we can only move through life as one who is spiritually disadvantaged. Many of our blind spots exist in the subconscious mind. Those blind spots can often take us off our highest path, and result in poor decisions based on old, unresolved traumas still held in the subconscious mind. These traumas do not even necessarily need to be severe, but simply enough to color our true vision of the world.

Light of the Eternal One naturally works on the subconscious mind even when performing the basic treatment, as the lines of energy flowing through the brain and nervous system in the basic treatment will impact the subconscious mind to some degree. However, if you want to accentuate your work on the subconscious mind, you can do so by performing a treatment with that specific intention. To do this, you would place your hands together as has been shown with relationship and situational treatments, your pinkies touching and palms facing upward. Then imagine your subconscious mind being held in the palm of your hands. You may want to envision your subconscious mind as an image of you when you were a child, that aspect of you that takes everything literally and does not question the nuances of language, or tone; that part of you that may still believe you are bad at something simply because you were once told that many years ago. Or, for some, you may want to imagine the subconscious as a small computer and that in performing the treatment on this aspect of yourself you are writing a new program on that computer.

However you want to envision your subconscious mind, see it being held in the palms of your hands. Then begin flowing Light of the Eternal One into that image of your subconscious mind held in your hands, knowing that as you do so you are actually flowing it into your subconscious mind. Do this for approximately five minutes, or until it feels as if the area above your hands is filled with light. When the treatment comes to an end, you may want to journal about your experience.

My own experience with this level of work is that I feel a cleansing of my subconscious, as well as old memories, both good and bad, emerging to the surface. Sometimes these are memories I have not thought of for decades, memories that may seem small and insignificant to my conscious mind, but which have emerged for a purpose. You can, if you wish, then do a follow-up treatment on that very memory, imaging that you are holding it in your hands as you did with the image of your subconscious mind, and then flowing Light of the Eternal One into it. In some cases, if this memory is of some kind of trauma, flowing Light of the Eternal One into that memory can help heal it, as the powerful light invokes a Divine presence that abolishes any sense of victimization, which in turn loosens the drama so that one can move ahead and be free of it once and for all.

This kind of work may not be for everyone, as some may prefer to let the basic treatment bathe and soothe any old injuries at the subconscious level over a period of time. And, eventually, working with just the basic treatment will do this. But, if you are like me and want to go right to the root of an issue, then performing treatments on the subconscious mind using Light of the Eternal One can help illuminate the deepest recesses of your subconscious, and assist in releasing old, unwanted patterns of behavior so that you can embrace your highest aspirations in life, instead of being ruled by your deepest traumas and fears.

20

Embracing the Greater We

You may have noticed that many of the treatments in this book are about relationship. The basic treatment works on your relationship to the Divine, and deepens that relationship so you can experience a deeper level of being one with the Divine. Then other treatments work on your relationship to significant people in your life, friends and family members, coworkers, and those who you interact with on a regular basis. Then the circle of working on relationship widened to include the many life forms in your neighborhood, the plant and animal kingdoms, and people who you may have never said hello to before. Suddenly, you began to notice that you are in relationship with everyone and everything. Also, you have worked on the relationship with various aspects of yourself, your higher self, and subconscious mind.

During all of this work on relationship, hopefully you have come to see, feel, and know the benefits of bathing these relationships with Light of the Eternal One. Hopefully, it has brought a sense of peace when there was turmoil, or illuminated other aspects of those relationships that you were previously unaware of and needed to see. Essentially, in performing these treatments we have been blessing these relationships by calling forth that underlying Divine light that supports the very existence of these relationships. And, by doing so, you have brought them closer to being in perfect alignment with the highest good. But this kind of relationship work does not need to end with the possible options and examples that have been mentioned in the previous chapters. You can and should take time to engage performing Light of the Eternal One treatments on all relationships that you are in, including to the most mundane as well as the most celestial items. And in doing so you will enter the paradigm of We, a mode of seeing that is relationship driven, and not driven by a consciousness concerned only with the self. The more you do this, the more you will begin to realize that you are in some form of relationship, albeit how great or small, with everything in the universe.

Begin by taking the time to honor your relationship to the sun, by performing a Light of the Eternal One relationship treatment on this relationship. As you do this, you may notice lines of light that exist directly between you and the sun. These lines of light are not rays of the sun, for you can sense them even when performing this treatment at night. These lines of light are like aspects of a Divine spiderweb that holds all creation together, that web that some refer to as the Divine matrix. In physics there is the concept called *string theory* that says everything at its most basic level is a line of energy. That energy, I believe, is Light of the Eternal One. And that Divine web that is holding the universe together is made of smaller parts of this energetic string.

What happens when you perform relationship treatments to what may appear to be random objects—such as the sun, or a doorknob—is that your consciousness is called directly into noticing the string, because that is probably what is most relevant for you to be aware of in that relationship: That binding universal light that is there between you and that other object.

The more I have worked with this concept, through energy experiments as well as through a form of meditation I call *Omega point meditation,* I have begun to notice at a deeper and deeper level how interwoven each action is with another's well-being, that no act is separate, isolated, or occurring in a vacuum. This mode of experimenting with consciousness can also be a mind-expanding meditation, in that you simply become aware that you are in relationship to everything that ever is, was, has been, or will be.

Being random in this kind of work actually helps you notice at a deeper level the lines of interconnection that are there. So, be random. Perform a treatment on your relationship to a spoon in the White House, or to a beggar's bowl in Bangkok, or to the star Cygnus X-1 (which happens to be a black hole), or anything and everything. The more you do this, the more your consciousness will gain an awareness of this cosmic spiderweb that is creation, that lines of light exist between you and the furthest item imaginable in the universe, and that on some level you are in relationship with that item.

As that Divine web begins to emerge in your awareness, you begin to notice how it impacts everything, that each act that you do is like a ripple going out to all those lines of light, even the ones that seem entirely insignificant. You become aware in this state of consciousness that you are in relationship to Christ on the cross and the Jewish Holocaust as you read this; that you are in relationship to each person who is starving, as well as each person who is in love; that you are in relationship to your ancestors and those who are yet to be born; and more, and more, and more.

Once this form of consciousness begins to be a backdrop for your thoughts, you can then begin to truly know the greater We that I have mentioned. The greater We in its largest form is that We that is all humanity, all animals, all plants, the collective consciousness of the entire planet. And the more you tune in to these lines of light that connect you to all things, which you can do by performing random Light of the Eternal One treatments on your relationship to even the most obscure things, then the more you begin to see the bigger picture, the growing consciousness that is larger than just yourself, or even the consciousness of humanity, but the consciousness of the entire planet striving to awaken.

But for some, even expanding your consciousness to be aware of the We that is simply humanity may be enough of a leap. That We that is the many nations, cultures, and people on this planet who are all intertwined, with one fate for all.

21

Lighting Up the Dreamtime

We are more than this physical form. And, there are realms of which we are part that exist far beyond our daily physical world. Some cultures refer to this collection of nonphysical realms as the *dreamtime*. For in dreaming, we reconnect with that aspect of ourselves existing in these nonphysical realms, and often interact there with other beings to share information, resolve issues, and even access spiritual power that awaits us in these other realms.

Most people relate to dreams through attempting to interpret them, or journaling about them. In Gestalt psychology, the theory is that you are everyone and everything in your dream. And often in that form of therapy individuals can make great strides in the success of their therapy by acting out their dreams, seeing each aspect of the dream as part of themselves. When using this form of dream acting as a therapy tool, individuals can often resolve issues that have haunted them for years.

I have a great deal of respect for Gestalt therapy, and for the dream work originated by its late founder,

Fritz Perls. But, I have also been exposed to amazing shamanic techniques for also working with dreams, most notably a technique by my dear, late shaman friend Carolion. As a teacher of her technique, I have been inspired to work with dreams in a new way by understanding that dreams can hold a great deal of spiritual power. That power can be revealed and retrieved to the dreamer by a properly trained shaman, or it can be empowered to the individual by using a Light of the Eternal One dream treatment.

To perform a Light of the Eternal One dream treatment, you first will want to recall as much of the dream as you can. You may want to keep a journal for this, and also know that it is possible to do a treatment on a dream fragment or dream that you do not entirely remember. Still, do your best to remember as much of the dream that you can.

Once you have a clear memory of the dream— or at least a portion or fragment of that dream— you then perform a Light of the Eternal One dream treatment, which essentially is a relationship treatment between you as the dreamer and the dream itself. To do this, you may want to take the page about the dream from your dream journal and hold it in your hands, using the same position as with previous Light of the Eternal One treatments of hands touching at the pinkies with palms facing upward. If you do not have a journal or written form of the dream, you can imagine that it is a movie being held in your hands. Also, imagine that you are sitting on the palm of your hands along with the dream, either watching the movie of your dream or reading the dream as it is written on the journal. Use whichever method works easiest for you. Now, flow Light of the Eternal One into not just the dream, but into *your relationship* to the dream, into your viewing of and experiencing of the dream.

As you flow this sacred light, which promotes a sense of oneness with the Divine in all things, including your dreams, know that you are shedding light not only on what the dream may want to reveal to you, but also on what power or spiritual gifts may latently exist for you within that dream.

At this point it is very important to trust your intuition. You may find that one of the characters or objects from the dream emerges strongly in your consciousness. If this happens, which is very likely, shift your intention so that you are now flowing Light of the Eternal One into your relationship to that character or object within your dream. You may even feel the character or object morph into something new, which is not uncommon. Still, keep flowing the light as this occurs.

Often, spiritual power is camouflaged within our dreams as something recognizable, so if there is a car door in your dream it could be that the car door in your dream is actually an energetic portal to a level of spiritual power you are now ready to access, and that it has nothing to do with being a literal car door. Try not to interpret the meaning of the dream, but to flow Light of the Eternal One into any areas of the dream that may seem emotionally charged for you, regardless of whether or not that charge makes any rational sense.

As Light of the Eternal One is flowing into the dream, it is uniting you with any aspects of your spiritual power you are ready to claim from the dream. Again, mentally interpreting the dream will not give you this same power. You must retrieve it energetically. Also, know that there may be some energies in your dream that you may not be meant to reclaim at this time. So, again, listening to your intuition is of utmost importance.

You can perform dream treatments repeatedly on the same dream. Do so if you are intuitively drawn to. Working with dreams in this way can retrieve spiritual power you have lost in this or other lifetimes, and can offer you the opportunity to positively shift your reality at the dreamtime level, which also impacts your life here in the physical world.

22

Preparing to Teach Light of the Eternal One

It is my hope that many who read this book will want to share Light of the Eternal One with others, not just as a treatment but also as an empowerment. Empowering others in this lineage offers them the opportunity to share this light, and widen the circle of healing to their friends and family as well. My hope is that like a chain reaction moving through the consciousness of humanity, this light would then quickly make a shift in the greater consciousness of the planet, and that greater We of which all of us are part. Soon, you will have the choice of whether of not to move ahead with the option of becoming empowered as a Light of the Eternal One teacher. For though you have yet to be empowered to initiate others into Light of the Eternal One, that empowerment is contained in the following chapter.

Before deciding whether or not to move ahead to the next level of this lineage, meditate on it. It may not be in everyone's highest path to be a teacher. You may simply want to be able to practice offering treatments without the responsibility of teaching this energy form to others. And that is entirely okay if that is your choice. But first, ask yourself what is in both your highest good and the highest good of the planet. Again, know that teaching is not for everyone, and that it is better to forgo teaching than it is to teach anyone halfheartedly or without true commitment.

You can, if you wish, even perform a situational treatment on this issue to assist you in your decision-making process. Simply imagine that you are holding in the palms of your hands the situation of your decision-making process on the question of you being a Light of the Eternal One teacher. As shown previously, your hands should be touching at the pinkies with palms facing the sky so that you really sense that you are supporting the issue, not grasping or crushing it. Now, flow Light of the Eternal One into that situation.

As you feel the energy flow, it is likely you may feel your answer emerge, as if it too is being held in the palms of your hands. Or, you may feel questions about your own abilities, or insecurities arise. Many things may come up in your consciousness as you do this, and it is important to listen to each layer of your consciousness being revealed as Light of the Eternal One takes you deeper and deeper into the issue at hand. It may be that you are not meant to teach this, and that instead you are meant to be devoting your time to other important things, such as being an artist, scientist, or doctor. And if that is the case, you may feel your calling to those other paths rise up in your consciousness as the energy is flowing. But hopefully, after the treatment you should have a basic idea of whether or not teaching Light of the Eternal One is right for you.

If you learn from the treatment that it is not your path to be teaching this energy form at this point in time, you can still learn more interesting energy techniques by reading the remainder of this book. And, if the answer to your question is that you should move forward with the teaching empowerment, then begin to prepare yourself for that undertaking.

My hope is that anyone teaching this system will take their commitment seriously and work diligently to improve their skills on a regular basis. Since there is no true regulating body for teaching energy work, often teachers in various energy-healing systems can range from being of a very high caliber to being very poor. Some have wonderful, supportive teaching skills, and others have few, if any. So, before going on to the empowerment for teaching Light of the Eternal One, prepare yourself by studying these guidelines for teaching energy work to help make you the best teacher you can be.

The first thing you need to have is integrity about your motivation for teaching. That means that you are honest in all of your interactions with students, and that you refuse to bring unnecessary personal agendas to the process of teaching. In other words, don't use your classes to try and make friends, find followers, or grow your own ego. If you teach a class of people, or individually, do so only because you believe in the energy and have a sincere desire to share this work with others. Do not pretend to know answers to some questions when you do not. There are too many teachers who fear saying *I don't know* when asked a question. Honesty is always better than false or half-informed answers. Always be true to your word, especially if your words are going to be taken as fact by the students who study with you.

Devote a significant amount of your time each week to improving your skills not only with the energy, but your people skills as well. During my first year as a Reiki Master, I wasn't that good at the simple people skills, such as making a person feel welcome when they arrived for a class or session. I was so focused on getting the energetic portion correct that I forgot about the basics of human interaction. If this is an area you may feel weak in, make a plan of what you might want to say to people when they arrive. Think of offering people something to drink, like tea or a glass of water. Such small things will go a long way to making a person feel welcome and at ease.

Have the utmost moral conduct with respect to your students and your life. If you cannot stand in alignment with the energy through your actions, then it is not in your or anybody else's highest good for you to take on this role. This also means you should not participate in any form of flirting or seductive behavior with respect to your students. Students can sometimes put you on a pedestal as the teacher, and that can also mean their affections can follow suit. Though it is fine to let someone admire you as a teacher, don't let it turn into anything beyond that.

Work on yourself, and then when you are done working on yourself, work on yourself some more. In other words, use this energy, or other energy forms you are trained in, to dig down into your deepest flaws, your most hidden blind spots, and heal them. Students will know and feel the commitment to your work even at the subconscious level simply by the way you carry yourself when teaching. If you have not worked on yourself, they will feel that and have less respect for you as a teacher, and less respect for the lineage itself. Please make a deep, lifetime commitment to your inner work.

Surrender to God, Goddess, the Divine by its many names. True teachers know that none of the gems of teaching come from them. We are only channels for a higher wisdom. The best teachers know how to get out of their own way. Encourage this in your students too. Teach them to depend on the Divine, not you, for their ongoing guidance.

Make a clear decision about the level at which you want to bring your commitment to teaching into your life. If you want to do it professionally, then treat it with the same level and care as you would any other profession. If, on the other hand, you are doing it simply to share this empowerment with friends and family, be clear about that as well. There is no right or wrong way, as long as you yourself know what your commitment truly is. But know that if you are uncertain about who you are as a teacher, students will sense that insecurity. Make a commitment one way or the other, knowing you can change that commitment as well if your life situation changes.

Dedicate a portion of your work for the good of the planet. If you are teaching on a regular basis, offer a gratis monthly or weekly group session where people can attend to work on sending Light of the Eternal One to issues around the planet.

Having read these guidelines, now journal about them. How does each guideline personally relate to you? How would you personally put each guideline into practice? This may seem like an undo amount of work to do before you receive the empowerment, but you should know that once you are empowered you will have the ability to teach. Now is the time to work out any kinks you may have emotionally, spiritually, or otherwise, with respect to being a teacher.

If you find that there are areas where you feel insecure about teaching, work on them by performing Light of the Eternal One situational treatments on these issues, holding that issue or situation of you as a teacher in your hands, and flowing Light of the Eternal One into it. Doing this for even one treatment can sometimes resolve the issue. If it takes repeated treatments, then continue working on the issue before you engage the empowerment in the following chapter. Know that there is no rush to get there, that this is not a race to see who can begin teaching Light of the Eternal One the fastest after reading these chapters.

If you feel ready to proceed immediately after reading this chapter, then trust your instinct. You very well may be ready, especially if you are already an established teacher of some other form of healing work, such as Reiki. However, if you do not feel ready, and want to take the next few weeks, or even months, preparing yourself, then take as much time as you need. There is no rush, no competition in this effort.

I also strongly encourage—through do not require—that anyone teaching this form of energy work make this book available as a reference. The reason I encourage it—as opposed to requiring it—is that I know that there will be situations where it will simply not be prudent to have the book available. But, since this book is the primary resource on this work, anyone teaching it in good faith should either do their best to provide copies during any trainings, or at least mention it as the primary reference.

I want everyone to know that what I am being told about Light of the Eternal One is that it is meant to travel quickly and grow exponentially so that the whole planet can reap the benefits of this work. It is a free energy system in the sense that it is not meant to be cumbersome to learn, or financially difficult to obtain training. It is based on tapping into something that is already a part of us, already sustaining us, as if we are simply tapping into those lines from the Bible in Genesis where God says, *Let there be light*. So, with that in mind, if you wish to be a teacher in this lineage, open to the next chapter, and let this light fill your life in ways far beyond what you have already known.

23

Embracing the Teaching Light

So, you want to be a Light of the Eternal One teacher. You have come this far, written about your experience in your journal, performed the basic treatment as well as situational/relationship treatments. Now you want to learn how to share this empowerment with others, so that their lives can be filled with this same light.

The teaching-level Light of the Eternal One empowerment is slightly different than the basic empowerment. It is different in that the teaching-level empowerment also involves your higher self. Please know and understand this, so that if you decide to teach more teachers of this lineage you give the appropriate empowerment. Also, one thing to note is that this empowerment was sent out by me while on the island of Bali, and also involves the inclusion energetically of a sacred holy spring in Bali called Tempak Sering. Those who are empowered directly by me through this book to the teacher level also receive this energetic cleansing that includes the energy of this sacred Balinese spring. This will add to the cleansing and purification process, and is not something you will be able to include in your own empowerments to others. It is simply something my guides informed me to do to add a higher level of cleansing to the teacher empowerment sent through this book.

Tempak Sering is a sacred spring in Bali where many Balinese go to wash away their sins, illness, or other such spiritual maladies. If I had been in France when writing this book, it is very likely I would have gone to the sacred waters of Lourdes for a similar effect. This book, though, was written in Bali, and I have incorporated the energy of this sacred water of Tempak Sering to give the empowerment a twenty-one-day cleansing cycle. Please do not let this discourage you from accepting the empowerment, nor let it imply that one has to subscribe to Balinese culture or the Hindu religion, which most Balinese subscribe to, in order to be a teacher of this lineage. I am, at heart, a pragmatic energy worker and usually rely upon that which is possible and available in my work. Please simply know that I included this sacred water in the empowerment to give the empowerment the deepest cleansing effect I could, given the spiritual tools available to me at the time.

The empowerment for the teacher level will instantly upgrade your energy system to be able to offer both the basic-level and teacher-level empowerments to others. It is also likely that after the empowerment you may feel a deep sense of euphoria or connection to the Divine. Be wise about the time and place you decide to engage this empowerment. You would be best suited to give yourself a full day to relish in this experience, and you may want to engage it at a time that feels sacred to you, perhaps a religious holiday or other day that holds a deeply spiritual significance for you.

When you have chosen the correct time and place, and are ready for the day of the empowerment, begin with a silent meditation. Perform a basic treatment on yourself, to deepen your sense of connection to the Divine. If you have any insights during this time about your path as a teacher, write them down or commit them to memory, as they are important messages that you are meant to carry with you on your journey as a teacher of this lineage. After performing the mediation and basic treatment on yourself, take a bath with a pinch of sea salt to cleanse your aura. Remain silent while you are bathing, again focusing on your path as a teacher, and what you hope to bring to that path. When you have finished bathing, dress silently in clothing that is suitable for this sacred occasion. You may decide to wear all white, or some other ritual form of dress. Do what feels right for you, as there is no one path to the Divine, nor just one way for you to express yourself appropriately through how you dress for this sacred empowerment. After dressing, light a candle to the Divine. And when you are ready, speak the following empowerment chant:

Blessed is all that is
Blessed is all that I am

I and my Higher Self now ask
for the Light of the Eternal One teacher
  empowerment
Blessings unto all
Blessings unto me

You may feel a tingling in your head as the empowerment moves down through your higher self, down into your crown chakra and fills your entire energy system. In this instant you are now a teacher of this sacred light. Behold the beauty of this day, and let the mystery of the cosmos sing to you. Take the rest of this sacred day to enjoy and relish in this blessed moment.

24

Teaching the Basic Level for Individuals

Teaching Light of the Eternal One is easy. It is meant to be easy, so that those who are empowered as teachers will regularly empower others in this wonderful, healing light. It is also meant to be easy so that it is not financially difficult for anyone to be trained in this modality, as full-day workshops can be costly. Any individual training at the basic level should not last more than one to two hours. You are now empowered to teach people either individually or in a group. However, I recommend teaching at least a few friends or family members individually first, just to create confidence in yourself as a teacher before you go on to teaching at the group level.

When teaching an individual, first let the person know beforehand to arrive for the empowerment already having taken a bath with sea salt, so that their aura is clean. Also, do your own part of preparation by lighting a candle to the Divine in the space where the empowerment will occur, and clearing the space by using a situational treatment on the room where the empowerment will occur.

You may even consider creating an altar in the room for this experience, if that feels suitable. Once the person arrives, offer a welcoming glass of water or herbal tea, to make the person feel welcome. Then, begin by talking about Light of the Eternal One and your own experience with it. Do not make this talk very long, however, as the Light of the Eternal One energy speaks for itself. The best way for people to understand the energy is to experience it directly.

Talk for ten minutes or so, sharing your personal experience with the energy and referencing this book as needed, then perform a basic-level treatment on the person you are about to empower. Do this in the typical manner by placing your hands on the top of their head while they are seated. Imagine seeing the person's head being filled with a waterfall of light that is coming down from the heavens, through your own head, into your hands, and into the person being treated. Hold your hands in this position for approximately five minutes, allowing the energy to fill their skull and entire nervous system.

When the five minutes is complete, or when you feel as if the person you are treating is filled with light, gently pull your hands away and allow the person to sit quietly to absorb the effect of the treatment. Since this is a teaching and not just you giving a treatment, in this instance I do recommend asking the person about their experience a few minutes after the treatment. Remember, when you are giving the treatment by itself, I do not recommend interrupting that space of quiet afterwards. However, for the purpose of gauging their understanding of the energy as one who is going to be empowered with it, you will want to both ask about their experience, as well as share your own experience as the one giving the treatment.

Tell them how you performed the treatment and anything about your own experience that you feel is relevant. And ask them what they felt, what they experienced, and validate their experience, whatever it may be. Remember, not everyone will feel the energy, though most people will. If the person did not feel the energy, simply validate that and also ask them how they feel now in the present moment. Most likely, they will mention feeling a deep sense of peace and calm, as even those who do not feel the energy as it flows still receive the calming benefit of the treatment. Give emphasis not to the feeling of the energy as it flows, but to the benefits of the treatment afterwards, which are primarily a deepening into the awareness of your own innate connection to the Divine.

Now, having given the person a sample of Light of the Eternal One, ask if they are ready to receive the empowerment, so that they can use this energy on themselves to deepen their own spiritual connection to the Divine, and to share this wonderful energy with family and friends. If the person says they are not yet ready, then do your best to answer whatever questions they may still have about the energy. Otherwise, proceed with giving the empowerment. Usually when I perform the empowerment I place my hands on top of the person's head, as if I were about to give them a basic treatment.

The empowerment you use for Light of the Eternal One comes through your higher self, which has been empowered at the teacher level to be able to upgrade other people's energy system so that they too can flow Light of the Eternal One. This empowerment is based on a technique that I have used in my books on Reiki and which is proven very effective for performing energetic initiations. The premise of this technique is that as long as you whisper your intention clearly, and then offer energy to your higher self through the form of breath, your higher self will perform the task at hand, as long as that task is for the highest good. Use the wording below, which is very specific to the intention of the empowerment. Then, blow three breaths at the end of the statement to activate the empowerment:

By the power of the golden light within
By the power of the sacred breath
I manifest this truth
I now will my Higher Self
to empower [name of person] and their energy system
to be able to flow Light of the Eternal One
for the remainder of this lifetime
I manifest this now with the assistance of all angels
  and beings of light
So be it!

(Blow three times to activate the empowerment)

Once you make that third breath as an offering to your higher self, you may feel as if there is an energy transfer happening about ten feet above your head. This is because that is exactly what is happening. Think of it as e-mailing an attachment that is uploaded to your higher self through the wording, and when you offer the three breaths it is like hitting the *send* button on your computer. That energetic attachment is then sent to the person you are empowering, about ten feet above their physical body, and then downloaded into their energy system. Having your hands on the person's head is more for symbolic purposes, and also provides a sense of comfort for some individuals. It is not required in order for the empowerment to work.

Once the empowerment is complete, gently slide your hands away from the person's head and allow them to bathe in this beautiful new energy. I generally will allow several minutes for them to just be in the feeling of the empowerment, which for some individuals feels like a deep sensation of spiritual bliss. When it feels right, go ahead and ask the person to place their own hands on top of their head and guide them through performing a basic treatment on themselves. Tell them to simply intend Light of the Eternal One to flow, and that it flows by intention. If they wish, they are welcome to visualize the waterfall of sparking white light coming down from the heavens through their hands into their head. But, know that the treatment happens by intention, and that the visualization is simply a way to allow their mind to participate at a deeper level. Some may not wish to visualize anything at all, and are willing to simply trust in the intent and flow of the energy. Be open as a teacher to go with what feels right for each individual. Do not press upon them one right or wrong way of doing this.

While the person is performing the basic treatment on themselves, remind them that they are filling up their skull with this Divine light, and that once the skull feels full of this energy, to then intend that it flow down their spine and throughout their entire nervous system. Again, some may not feel the energy as it is flowing, so for them simply monitor the treatment so that they flow the energy for approximately five minutes. Since Light of the Eternal One has its own Divine intelligence, it will flow down the spine and through the nervous system on its own, even if the person is not energetically sensitive enough to intentionally guide the energy in this manner.

When the five minutes is finished, or when the person indicates that they feel filled with the light, tell them to gently bring their hands down in a restful position and to simply meditate on the sensation of peace that Light of the Eternal One evokes. Give them space to enjoy this feeling, this deepening of their place of oneness with the Divine. Then, after several minutes, ask them if they want to share anything about their experience. Again, since this is a teaching, it is important that they know how to articulate their own experience about the energy as one who will now be able to facilitate treatments for others.

Once the person has shared about their experience, guide them through offering a basic treatment on you, so that they have the experience of giving a treatment to another person. Have them stand behind you and place their hands gently on top of your head. Then, tell them to simply intend that Light of the Eternal One flow through their hands into your head. Encourage that if it feels right to them, they can visualize the waterfall of light coming down from heaven, through the top of their head, down their hands, and into you. Remind them that the visualization is not required, but simply gives active minds an avenue of participation in the process.

Tell the person to either flow the energy for five minutes, or to monitor the energy if they are energy sensitive. If they are energy sensitive, they should try to sense when it feels as if your head has filled with light. Once this happens, tell them to intend that it then flow down your spine and throughout your entire nervous system. Again, if they are not energy sensitive, reinforce for them that that has nothing to do with the level of their spirituality, and that it is simply a kinesthetic sense, like any other sense with varying degrees of accuracy. And then remind them to just flow the energy for approximately five minutes.

Whatever you do, do not shame anyone for not being able to feel the energy. I have seen this happen too many times in New Age healing circles, where some people are told by the facilitator and others all kinds of horrible things about why they cannot feel the energy. My own experience is that some of the most spiritual and loving people I know cannot feel Reiki, Light of the Eternal One, or any other form of energy healing. And yet these are very spiritual people. Similarly, I have known some individuals on my journey who are very adept at sensing things energetically, who are at the same time quite manipulative and not living their lives from a place of spiritual integrity. Please do not label anyone as not being spiritual simply because they are not energy sensitive. The two items are not related.

When the treatment comes to an end, after the five minutes or after they sense that you have filled with the light, tell them to gently pull their hands away from your head. Remind them that in most situations, they should give the person receiving the treatment space at this point, and not ask questions about the experience. Since this is a teaching session, however, feel free to invite their questions, as well as their own point of view about the experience. Take as much time as is needed to discuss the experience, then move ahead with the process of teaching them the *opening the path to love* treatment, wherein the hand position is to hold the hands over the heart instead of the head. Teaching this simple variation should not take much time, but you may want to give them time to reflect on how it feels differently than the basic treatment. Ask them if they notice a difference between the two treatments, and let them know as well about the option of combining the two treatments into one, with one hand on the head and the other over the heart. Make sure to let them know that for some people, the combined treatment can be overwhelming.

Next, teach the situational/relationship treatment option. Begin by asking the person if they have a relationship, or a situation in their lives, which can use some energetic assistance. Most people will have at least one, if not more, relationship or situation issue they can work on. But if for some reason the person cannot think of anything, have them perform a relationship treatment on one of their parents. There is always going to be something that can be learned by performing such a treatment.

Once a situation or relationship has been decided upon, teach the simple hand position for this treatment. Have the person hold out their hands, pinkies touching with palms facing the sky. Encourage any use of imagery for the person to visualize the relationship or situation in the palm of their hands. I relate to the idea of a feather, which reinforces the idea of lightness and an ability to fly. It may be, though, that a flower or seed or other such image works better for the person. Trust your intuition when working with them at this level of the treatment, for it is important for them to believe that the situation or relationship really is being held in their hands on some level.

Having found an appropriate image, now instruct them to flow Light of the Eternal One from their hands into that image, which will directly carry the energy into the situation or relationship being worked on. You may, if you are someone who is energy sensitive, feel the energy flow even though it is not directed at you. For some people, this is normal and will simply result in a residual sensation of receiving a small amount of Light of the Eternal One as a by-product of being present during the treatment. If this happens for you, simply think of it as an added bonus for teaching this wonderful gift to another person.

As the energy continues to flow, you may want to ask the person if they sense anything energetically, or any shifts in consciousness around the situation or relationship being treated. Even if they are not energy sensitive, it is very likely they will have a shift in consciousness, a new and more understanding perspective on the relationship or situation. Ask them to voice their experience, so that by speaking about their experience it reinforces for them that the treatment is having an impact. When the five minutes are up, or when it feels as if the area above the person's hands is saturated with light, guide the person into ending the treatment by having them gently pull their hands apart so their hands can rest in their lap or at their sides.

At this point, you can again ask them if there is anything they want to share about their experience of performing a relationship or situational treatment. There very well may be things they feel more comfortable sharing now that the treatment is over and they can focus simply on the discussion. Allow this discussion to unfold, and always validate their experience, whatever it may be. Even if they felt nothing at all during the treatment, not even a shift in consciousness, ask them to simply notice any changes that may occur with respect to that issue over the coming days or weeks. But never indicate that they should have felt something they didn't feel, nor imply that somehow they are lacking because they didn't sense anything. Their own pace with this work has to be respected, so be patient and simply reinforce for them that the real test is when changes begin to occur in their life, not simply whether or not they feel some immediate energetic sensations during the treatment.

Once you have completed training them how to perform a basic self-treatment, a treatment on another, and a situational/relationship treatment, reinforce the importance of performing the basic treatment each day for forty days. The forty-day cycle allows the treatments to have a combined cumulative effect, which will cause a permanent shift in the person's consciousness and energetic system, a shift that will allow them to experience a place of oneness with the Divine more easily on a daily basis. It is not that all will be lost if they do not perform the forty-day cycle of basic treatments, but simply that they will evolve at a faster and deeper level with the energy if they do follow the forty-day cycle after being empowered with the energy.

At this point you can also share any of your own stories about how the forty-day cycle impacted you. Tell them of any significant changes you noticed in your own life. Again, the more true, personal stories you can bring to the teaching, the better it will be for you as a teacher as well as for the student. Also, suggest the option of keeping a journal during this forty-day period. Journaling does not change the energetic aspect of the treatments, but it can assist many people in grounding their experience, as well as provide a reference and document of the changes they may go through during this profound and life-changing forty days.

Having now empowered the individual and shown them the treatment options at the basic level, you can now bring the training to a close by asking if there are any final questions. If there are, simply answer the questions to the best of your ability. Remind the person that Light of the Eternal One is a simple and user-friendly form of energy that does not require an in-depth knowledge of chakras, meridians, or other aspects of the human- energy system. Even just the basic treatment can bring about real life change if repeated daily over a period of forty days. Give emphasis to the simplicity of this system: That is the beauty of it.

One final thing to do before the person leaves is to thank them for giving you the opportunity to perform the empowerment. If they do not have your contact information, feel free to give it to them. But, letting go is part of the trust a teacher must have in their student. If they have further questions, let them come to you. Otherwise, trust that the real teacher for them will be the energy itself and the Divine. Know that you have done your part by bringing this wonderful light to another. Know, also, that sometimes giving the empowerment to another can instill a sense of blissful euphoria similar to when you receive the empowerment. Relish any deepening of your own relationship to the Divine that may occur by being a vessel to share this sacred light with others.

After the student leaves the room where the empowerment has occurred, go ahead and offer your thanks to the Divine for the opportunity to give this empowerment, and then delicately and with reverence extinguish the candle you lit earlier to the Divine. In extinguishing the candle, know that the light you have just now helped bring to the life of another will shine much brighter than any candle. Take the remainder of the day to rest and be kind to yourself, for in sharing this sacred light with another, you have done a wonderful deed.

25

Teaching the Basic Level to Groups

Teaching Light of the Eternal One to groups is not that different than teaching it to an individual. However, I recommend teaching at the group level only after you have taught several people at the individual level to instill a sense of confidence in your abilities. Once you feel ready, trust that you are. But know that there is no rush to teach at the group level, and that for some teachers the preference may always be to teach only individually. Whatever your preference is, there is not one way that is better than the other. There are these two options to suit the different needs of both teachers and students.

Group teaching can be in a very formal, professional setting, such as in an advertised two- or three-hour workshop, or in a less formal setting, such as a gathering of friends or family. But in both of these possibilities the core of the teaching is the same. As with the individual basic-level class, you need to prepare all students by informing them to take a bath with a pinch of sea salt prior to attending. This cleanses their aura and helps set a sacred tone for their day. It is important as well that you, as the teacher, also take such a bath, and that you clear the space where the class will be held using the situational treatment of Light of the Eternal One on the room. After this, prepare the space with an altar to the Divine, if that feels appropriate, or, at a minimum, at least light a candle to the Divine. You may also want to provide some tea and water, or light, healthy snacks so that people feel welcome as they arrive. A final suggestion is to have this book available for purchase at the class, since it is the primary resource on this form of energy work. If you are not able to make the book available for those in the class, you may want to at least suggest it to them as recommended reading.

Once everyone has arrived and is seated for the class, you may want to have a brief period for students to introduce themselves to the group. This should be kept to only a few minutes so that it does not steal time and energy from the task at hand. If someone is talking too long about themselves, or going off on an unrelated subject, try to easily nudge them to focus on a brief explanation of why they are here and anything they may want to share about what drew them to the class. Once the introductions come to an end, share a little about yourself, focusing on your experience with Light of the Eternal One and any other background information about you that is relevant to the class. If it is not relevant, then don't mention it. This time is for teaching, and that should be the primary focus.

After talking about your own experience with the energy, prepare the group to receive the basic Light of the Eternal One treatment from you. Generally, try your best to offer each person an individual treatment. If performing each treatment individually, begin by asking everyone in the room to keep their eyes closed, and to simply focus on their own connection to the Divine. Then start to your left and walk clockwise around the group, performing the basic treatment on each person, one person at a time. When the treatments have all come to an end, invite everyone in the room to open their eyes and then have a short group sharing about the experience.

If the size of the group is too large, and you feel the process of offering everyone an individual treatment may take too long, there is a shortcut you can use. The shortcut for sending the basic-level treatment to an entire group of people at once is to simply intend that your knees represent the head of each person in the room. Start with everyone seated, including yourself. Before you begin the treatment, ask that everyone close their eyes and focus on their connection to the Divine. Then, bring your hands down so that one hand is on each knee, and simply intend the energy to flow. As Light of the Eternal One is flowing from your hands into your knees, it is also flowing into everyone's head in the room, filling up their skull with this Divine light. Let the energy flow for approximately five minutes, adding any appropriate visualization of this sparkling white light coming down from above, flowing through their heads at the crown, down their spine, and throughout their entire nervous system. When the treatment comes to an end, let everyone know that they can open their eyes. Then have a little time for group sharing about their experience.

To begin the sharing, simply announce to the group that now is a good time to share if anyone cares to offer insights about their own experience. Lay down some ground rules to focus the sharing, so that only one person at a time is speaking. This is to keep people from cross-talking, which can invalidate the experience of those who may not feel as strong in their opinion, especially if they get interrupted. Remind everyone to keep their sharing simple and to the point, as sometimes in these situations group sharing can disintegrate and go off topic. Keep the sharing to a few minutes, and then speedily move ahead to the empowerment.

The basic-level empowerment can be performed either individually on each person in the group one at a time, or you can do it en masse for the entire group. Again, trust your instinct as to which method is right for your group. If the group is small and intimate, you may be best suited by doing each empowerment individually. To do this, first invite everyone to close their eyes. Then go around, one person at a time, placing your hands on the top of each person's head and use the empowerment chant to pass the empowerment from your higher self to that individual before moving on to the next individual. You can do this by using the empowerment chant as written in the previous chapter. Once you have completed empowering everyone in the group, allow a few minutes for the group to relish this moment and deepen into the often blissful sensation it brings.

Then, when it feels appropriate, move ahead with the next stage of teaching everyone how to perform a basic treatment on themselves. Again, for small and intimate groups, this method of working on each person individually is most likely the best way to perform the empowerment, as it has a more personal touch.

However, if you are working with a large group and feel that performing the empowerment one person at a time will make some people restless as they wait, then there is the option of empowering the entire group simultaneously. To do this, first invite everyone to close their eyes. Then, bring your hands together with pinkies touching, palms facing up to the sky, and intend that you are holding the entire group in your hands. Once you feel as if you are holding the entire class in your hands, whisper the following invocation to activate the empowerment from your higher self to everyone in the group.

> *By the power of the golden light within*
> *By the power of the sacred breath*
> *I manifest this truth*
> *I now will my Higher Self*
> *to empower everyone in this group and their energy*
>   *systems*
> *to be able to flow Light of the Eternal One*
> *for the remainder of this lifetime*
> *I manifest this now with the assistance of all angels*
>   *and beings of light*
> *So be it!*

(Blow three times to activate the empowerment)

You may feel a huge amount of light enter the room at this moment, as everyone's energy system is simultaneously upgraded. Allow a few minutes for the group to relish this moment and deepen into the blissful sensation it brings. Then, when it feels appropriate, move ahead with the next stage of teaching everyone how to perform a basic treatment on themselves.

Teaching the basic self treatment in groups is the same, whether or not you empowered the group individually or as a whole. Begin by simply inviting everyone to place their hands on top of their head and intend that Light of the Eternal One flow into their skull, and then down their spine through their entire nervous system. Describe the energy as a waterfall of light flowing down from the heavens, but emphasize that all that is required for the energy to flow is the simple intention of the practitioner. Also, remember to let the group know that not everyone will necessarily feel the energy flowing, and that even those who may not feel the energy flowing will still receive the benefits of the treatment. Describe these benefits as a sense of deeper connection to the Divine, a sense of peace and wholeness, and a quieting of the mind. Remind everyone that the benefits of the treatment are the reason for performing it, and that any sensations one may or may not feel around the energy actually flowing are secondary.

Keep an eye on the group and also keep note of the time. After the group has performed the treatment for approximately five minutes, invite everyone to bring down their hands and rest them in their lap or at their side. Allow a few minutes of silence, and then let everyone know that for the deepest benefit to be gained, it is best to perform the basic self-treatment daily for forty days straight, and that journaling about their forty-day cycle can have the added benefit of grounding their feelings and documenting their experience. Then, offer an invitation for group sharing about their experience of giving themselves the basic treatment.

Remember, you will want to keep the discussion focused on the topic. Remind everyone to speak only for their own experience, and not to interrupt others while they are talking. Depending on the size of the group, you may need to consider setting a time limit for the sharing to occur. If you decide to do this, announce it beforehand so that everyone understands the time frame for the sharing.

Once the sharing is complete, move ahead with the next stage of the training and teach everyone how to perform a basic treatment on somebody else. Divide the group into pairs for this stage of the training. If the group total is an odd number, invite someone to be your partner for the teaching. When you have divided the whole room into pairs, ask that they decide between themselves who will give a treatment first and who will receive. Then, talk them through the treatment, starting with the gentle placement of hands on the other person's head. Inspire them with a keen visualization of the waterfall of light coming down from the heavens, through their hands, and into the head of the person they are working on. But also remind them that what is most important is their intention that the energy flow, even if they do not see or feel the waterfall of light you speak of.

After several minutes into the treatment, ask if they have any sensation of the other person's head having filled with light, and remind them that if that has happened, to now intend that the light flow down the person's spine and through their entire nervous system. Also be inclusive of those who may not sense the energy, and let them know that the energy has its own intelligence and will do what is needed at the right time. When it feels like everyone who is receiving a treatment is filled with light, or after approximately five minutes, invite those giving the treatment to withdraw their hands from their partner's head and sit quietly while their partner fully absorbs the treatment in silence.

Obviously, you must break the silence after several minutes, since this is a training and not just an individual session. Do this by quietly asking everyone in the room to change roles with their partner. Then, repeat the process above so that the second half of the room has the opportunity to perform a basic treatment on their partner as well. After both partners have given and received a treatment, invite them to share about their experience with each other. Allow about ten minutes for this sharing to occur, then invite just a few comments from the group. Add any comments of your own that you may feel are relevant, and then move on to teaching the group how to perform the *opening the path to love* treatment.

Teaching the *opening the path to love* treatment should only take a few minutes, as it is simply an adjustment on the hand position from the head to the heart. Allow the group to experience this form of treatment by performing it on the same partner they just worked with. Once everyone in the room has had a chance to both give and receive this form of treatment, again have some time for sharing between partners. Then, when the sharing has come to an end, let everyone know about the option of combining this treatment with the basic treatment by placing one hand on the head and the other on the heart. *But do not have the group practice this during the class, since for some people it will be overwhelming.* Simply let them know it is a very powerful option, one that some people would not prefer and that others would. Then, move on to teaching the situational/relationship treatment.

For this portion of the training, first explain the proper position of hands touching at the pinkies, with palms open facing the sky, as if they are gently and lovingly holding a feather or a flower. Then, invite the group to imagine either a situation they are part of, or a relationship in their own lives they want to work on. Let them know that by *relationship,* this can also include their relationship to their boss, coworkers, friends, family members, and others. It does not have to be about an intimate relationship. Also, this is a good time to remind them that by sending energy to the situation or relationship, they are not sending it directly to any individuals.

Give emphasis that to send energy directly to an individual should require their consent. This is important for them to understand, so that they do not go around randomly sending energy to everyone they know, which would be an invasion of other people's energetic space and privacy.

Ask if everyone has a situation or relationship they want to work on. If someone does not, you can recommend they work on their relationship with one of their parents, and remind them that there is always something to be gained by doing this. Let them know that performing this Light of the Eternal One relationship treatment on the relationship with one of their parents reinforces a deeper knowledge and understanding of their own lineage, even if there are no real issues to be worked out with that specific parent.

Once you know that everyone in the room has a situation or relationship they want to work on, invite everyone to imagine that situation or relationship being gently held in the palm of their hands like a feather. Then, guide the group to begin flowing Light of the Eternal One into that feather, knowing that as the energy flows from their hands it is actually flowing into that relationship or situation the person is intending to work on.

Encourage each person in the room to hold this flow for five minutes, even if it brings up deeper issues. After the five-minute period is up, invite everyone to let go of the imagined feather and rest their hands in their lap or by their side. Then, invite a group sharing about the experience.

If there is time remaining, after teaching the basic self-treatment, treatment on another, and situational/relationship treatment, ending with some energetic play is always a good way to bring things to a close. I say this because often people can be very stiff when it comes to learning energy work. Some people have a great deal of fear, due to negative conditioning from some religions (and science) about the entire concept that human beings can access Divine energy, or even direct it to an issue, for that matter. Loosen up the group by encouraging their own sense of playfulness with the energy. These exercises can only be done in a group, and so take advantage of this opportunity to share them.

The first energy exercise I like to show is to get everyone on a circle, with their hands on the back of the person to each side, as if they are holding the back of the person's heart both to the right and left of them. Once all hands are on the back of everyone's heart chakra, begin flowing Light of the Eternal One as a group. The group impact exponentially raises the overall power of the energy. You may feel like a beam of light is now shooting through your heart from the back, going out in front of you into infinity. Whenever I perform this exercise with a group, inevitably we all eventually burst out laughing.

Another exercise I recommend is having the entire group perform a relationship treatment on the group's relationship to itself. Often, this can lead to individuals suddenly feeling more connected as a group, and will sometimes even start new friendships between people who didn't even speak to each other before this exercise began.

Be imaginative and try to find some exercises of your own that you would like to share with the group if there is time. Whatever options you use, keep it light and let people know that playing with the energy can make them feel at ease with it, which increases the possibility of them really integrating Light of the Eternal One into their lives.

Always end the class by giving thanks to everyone for the opportunity of sharing this blessed gift with them, and encourage them to contact you if they have future questions. Then, once everyone has departed the room, give thanks to the Divine for this wonderful gift, and reverently put out the candle you lit earlier in honor of the Divine.

26

Empowering Others
to Teach

Teaching Light of the Eternal One can be a great joy in life, and empowering others to be able to expand this circle of light by becoming teachers is an even greater joy. As I mentioned earlier, Light of the Eternal One is simple to learn so that it will be accessible to all. This is also true for the teaching level.

When someone approaches you about learning to be a teacher in this lineage, it is very likely that they may have already been your student for the basic-level training. But if they are not, interview them about their own experience with Light of the Eternal One. Ask them what they learned about themselves during the forty-day cycle, and how they have used the energy on themselves and others. This interview is not intended to make it difficult for others to attain the teacher level, but at least some level of screening to make sure the person has actually been trained to the basic level is appropriate.

Once you feel confident that the person has both been properly empowered to the basic level, and has completed the forty-day cycle, schedule a mutually agreeable time for training to begin. Remind the person to make sure they arrive for the training having taken a bath with a pinch of sea salt for cleansing their aura. Also, make sure that you properly prepare the space where the training will occur by performing a situational treatment on the room just prior to the training. Light a candle to the Divine before the student arrives, or even create a more embellished altar to the Divine. The choice is yours.

When the student arrives, greet them with a welcoming offer of water or tea to instill a sense of graciousness on your part as the teacher. Then, share some of your own thoughts about what it means to be a teacher in this lineage and about your journey with Light of the Eternal One. Speak straight from the heart, as that is the best way to convey your truth about what teaching this form of energy work means to you. After sharing, invite any questions the person may have about teaching. Some of these questions may not be answerable until after they have the empowerment, but most will. Answer their questions to the best of your ability, remembering that it is better to admit not knowing an answer than it is to fabricate one. When it feels like their questions have been exhausted, move ahead with giving the empowerment.

To perform the empowerment, you will use a chant similar to the one you used to empower individuals at the basic level. This chant will send the teacher-level empowerment from your higher self to their higher self, and down into their physical being, activating their entire energy field to be at the teacher level. You may want to describe this to the person, so that they then know exactly what is happening during the empowerment. Also, both from a spiritual and attributive point of view, it is important to acknowledge the source of the chant, and this book that the chant is contained in, since the student will need to learn the chant themselves in order to fully empower others in this lineage.

When you are ready to give the empowerment, ask the student to be seated if they are not seated already. Then, stand behind them, resting your hands gently on the top of their head. Now, speak the empowerment chant below to activate this transfer of energy.

> *By the power of the golden light within*
> *By the power of the sacred breath*
> *I manifest this truth*
> *I now will my Higher Self*
> *to empower*
> *and their Higher Self*
> *to the Light of the Eternal One teacher empowerment*
> *for the remainder of this lifetime*
> *I manifest this now with the assistance of all angels*
> *and beings of light*
> *So be it!*

(Blow three times to activate the empowerment)

After the third breath, gently withdraw your hands from the student's head. Then, sit quietly for several minutes as the student experiences the usually blissful sensation of having received this empowerment. When you sense that the student has had enough time to deepen into the sensations of the empowerment, begin to explain the empowerment process. Teach them the empowerment chants for both the basic and teacher level, and describe the process to the best of your ability how the empowerment actually moves from their higher self to the person being empowered. This is the easy part, as the empowerment chants are simple to learn and to perform. And sharing this knowledge with the student shouldn't take much time at all.

Then, have the student practice giving the empowerments on you, as though you are their student. Allow them to try this for both the basic and teacher level. For each level, have them talk through all the steps, such as informing you to take the cleansing bath with sea salt before you arrive, and their own necessary preparations, such as clearing the space energetically and lighting a candle to the Divine.

If they miss any of the steps, simply remind them of the step they missed and then encourage them to continue. Once they have talked through all the steps prior to the empowerment, have them actually perform the empowerment on you as if you were their new student. Even though you are already empowered, you are likely to still feel the euphoric sensations after each empowerment. And, as simple as each empowerment is to perform, it is still important for the student to practice it on you so they have the feeling of having actually done the work. Make sure that you mention any sensations that you may feel after each empowerment, as this validates to the student that the energetic transfer was real.

Now, have the student verbally repeat back to you the process for each empowerment as well the preparatory steps leading up to the empowerments. Once you sense that they have a clear understanding of the empowerment process for each level, ask them to repeat back to you the information that would need to be covered were they actually teaching a class. Feel free to quiz them and make sure they know their information correctly. Once you feel confident that they sufficiently understand all the information they would need to convey to their future students, ask them if they have questions about anything related to being a teacher, setting up classes, or how they can be supportive of their own students in the future. Do your best to answer any question that arises and also express to them that they can contact you if further questions or issues arise after the training. Being available as a mentor to a new teacher is always important, as often they cannot know the areas they may get stuck until they begin teaching, and that is when your support can be most helpful to them.

Once you and the student feel that the student is fully empowered and has a good foundation to move ahead with teaching on their own, thank them for choosing you as their teacher and for the opportunity to empower them to this sacred light. Also, make sure you give them your contact information should they need further support and mentoring in the future. When the student departs the room where the empowerment has taken place, give gratitude to the Divine and reverently put out the candle previously lit in honor of the Divine. And relish the blessing it is to have shared the teacher-level empowerment with another human being.

Teaching and Certifying Others

One item that may come up while empowering others at either the basic or teacher level is the issue of certification. On some level, this is uncharted territory to have a book be the primary document that authorizes others to teach. However, if we had had a similar book for Reiki from the founder Mikao Usui, or other books that could resolve the mysteries that sometimes occur when a tradition has no primary written source, then a lot of confusion and misinterpretation that has happened with Reiki and other systems could have been avoided.

Everything my guidance tells me about Light of the Eternal One is that there are to be as few obstacles as possible for it to travel swiftly from one person to the next, like a chain reaction in the consciousness of humanity, bringing a deeper sense of peace and spiritual presence for humanity as a whole. For the above reasons I have come to conclude that certification is something that you can offer for either level if you are willing to, depending on how formal and professional you want to be about teaching.

There is no written authority for this lineage other than this book. If you learn from this book, you are learning from the most direct source, unless you have studied with me personally. Also, you have the empowerment that has been sent from my higher self, as well as more information than I could possibly cover in a full-day workshop. And, it is my belief that the steps for both offering treatments and empowering others are so incredibly simple I cannot imagine anyone getting these steps wrong. Therefore, I offer my blessing to anyone who wishes to take the time to offer certificates to others, as long as that certificate mentions this book as the source for this work. Below is a sample of how such a certificate might look for the basic level:

> *This certifies that John Doe*
> *has received the basic-level training*
> *in Light of the Eternal One spiritual healing system*
> *as sourced from the book*
> *Energy Healing for Everyone channeled by Brett Bevell*
> Date_____ Facilitator_____

It is easy to get your own certificates printed, even if just on your own computer using nice paper with a colorful border for the printing. This would keep any costs low, and yet still offer those students who desire certificates to have them. If you feel called to offer certificates as a teacher, or have students who are asking for them, then please go ahead and offer them if it feels right to you. And, if it doesn't feel right to you, there is certainly no requirement that certificates be offered, especially in cases when the teaching occurred for free.

Creating an Abundant Life

Abundance is our birthright. By abundance, I mean having enough of what you need in life to be joyful and happy. In some ways, this is tricky territory to navigate, as some religions imply that poverty is the path to God, and some New Age writings act as if the only way to be happy is to be able to manifest all your material desires. For me, neither of these options appropriately expresses the utmost path to the Divine. Light of the Eternal One offers the opportunity to create abundance in your life, an abundance that is not limited to material desires, but one that is more guided by your relationship to the Divine to open new opportunities into your life, bring meaningful friendships, good health, and also enough financial support for you to achieve your life purpose.

The way you can begin to work on this spiritual expression of abundance is first by committing to another forty-day cycle of working just on this specific issue. Perform a daily basic treatment each day, as you did with the first forty-day cycle. During the basic treatment you do nothing different than before, as your intention for that treatment should simply be to deepen your relationship to the Divine. But, once you complete the basic treatment each day, you then perform a situational treatment on your path of abundance in this life.

To perform such a treatment, place your hands together side by side, touching at the pinkies with palms facing the sky. Then, imagine a miniature of yourself sitting in the palms of your hand. Embellish this self not necessarily with material goods, but visualize this self as the person that you truly want to be. Include having the financial freedom you need to live the life you want, but do not make that the primary goal. The goal should be your own inner happiness and fulfilling the promise of your life.

Fulfilling the promise in life may mean that you need a new job, more money, or other material items that will assist you in reaching that goal. But, if you make those objects the focus of your work, and are not focusing on the deeper aspect of what those material items may bring, then you are missing the point. Stay focused on that miniature you sitting in the palm of your hands, having all that you need in order to fulfill your promise in life. Then, begin to flow Light of the Eternal One through your hands, into that image, knowing that you are flowing this energy toward the situation of manifesting that life for yourself, that life where you have what you need and are living your life on purpose. Keep the treatment focused for approximately five minutes, and then give thanks to the Divine and let your hands rest when the five minutes comes to an end.

If you do this for forty days, simply doing your basic treatment each day, followed by the situational treatment just described, doors will open in your life that will give you what you need to have *real abundance*. And I say real abundance because simply satisfying material desires is not the true goal of any spiritual path. When you perform the treatment above, it allows the Divine to bring to you what you *truly need*, which may be more important than what you *think you need*. As part of that, it will open doors to enrich your life so that you have the financial freedom necessary to create your life's purpose. And that includes the financial freedom you also need to be maintain good health, and to explore whatever you need to explore in life to sustain the life you were meant to live. This kind of abundance also includes an abundance of real friendships, and abundance of well-being and happiness. This is what I mean by real abundance, as opposed to the imaginary abundance of simply satisfying another material desire that may or may not help you in the bigger journey of your soul.

Just as there are some people who may not feel comfortable asking for what they need to live life on purpose, as opposed to asking for specific material goals, there are also going to be some people who will want to sidestep the very issue of abundance. I have met such people quite often on my journey as a healer and teacher, and I know them well because I used to be one of them. Those are the people who probably need this work the most.

I say this because for years I had a wealth of spiritual knowledge that I did not share with others, because I was spending my life living frugally, and worked so much to make ends meet that I did not have the time to teach classes, nor the money to advertise workshops, nor the time to really write books. Yet, whenever anyone would speak to me about poverty consciousness I would scoff at the idea that perhaps I suffered from it. But the fact is I did suffer from a kind of consciousness that thought being spiritual meant being poor, a consciousness that would not allow me to ask for what I needed in life to do the work I was meant to do. Luckily, I eventually healed that aspect of my consciousness.

I mention this now because there will be some who read this book who may find a great deal of the information in this book very helpful, who will want to stop reading once they get to this chapter. When they get here, it will make them look at that aspect of their consciousness and they will not want to. So to those people, I simply ask you to try the forty-day cycle for creating abundance in your life. It cannot hurt you. It is not focused primarily on material goods and does nothing to promote greediness. It simply offers the opportunity to get what you need to live your life on purpose.

If you perhaps feel that you are someone who is suffering from a kind of poverty consciousness and blocking your own path of abundance, you can also add an additional treatment to the process of the forty-day cycle for abundance. The treatment you will add is simply to perform a Light of the

Eternal One treatment each day on your relationship to money. This treatment will help release any negative programming you may have about money so that you can learn to see it as neither something to crave nor avoid, but simply as an energy coupon, a coupon that represents the efforts of our labor. Seeing money in this way can help free you from the many addictions and compulsions around money that some people have.

During the forty-day cycle, you may also want to keep a journal. In this journal, write down what true abundance means to you. Write in detail the life you want to live, including every aspect of that life, and not simply the material possessions or amount of money in the bank account that are so often associated with abundance. You may find that the deeper you go into this work, ideas will come to you about actions you can take to improve your life, to help you feel more abundant about yourself. The more abundant you feel about yourself, the more you will draw situations to you that help create more of that abundance.

This work may even translate into how you decide to offer Light of the Eternal One treatments or classes to others. It may be that you feel enough abundance in your life that you want to share this gift freely with others, as a kind of service work for the greater good. Or, it may be that you begin to see how a path exists for creating abundance in your life by teaching classes and offering treatments for a modest and reasonable fee. Neither path is right or wrong, but both paths exist and will be influenced by your own attitudes on abundance. Whatever you decide, let that decision come from the work you do on having an abundant life, and know that there are many ways to interpret what abundance is as long as it leads to you living an empowered, happy, and purpose-filled life.

The Divine wants us to be happy and live life joyfully. Performing the forty-day cycle of treatments for abundance will help you find the abundance you need to live such a life. You hold that future you want in your hands when performing these treatments. Own that future. Relish it. Cherish it. Let the love of the Divine flow through all that you are, including your work, your finances, but also your health, your friendships, and all aspects of you that coalesce into that feeling of being abundant in all areas of your life.

Living Community

My years of spiritual exploration have shown me that true spirituality must involve community. The spiritual quest cannot exist in a void. True, there may be times when it is necessary to retreat away from the world and go inward, but if that inwardness never reaches a place of seeing and acknowledging the Divine interconnectedness of all things, and never translates into actions that help others, then an element of spiritual sincerity within that quest is missing. Conversely, I do not mean that in order to live a spiritual life that you have to join a commune, or associate only with those of like spiritual mind. Such rigid thinking is the basis of many cults that cannot tolerate spiritual diversity. The spiritual community I speak of is simple, and acknowledges both the differences as well as the similarities among peoples' various spiritual journeys. This form of community brings people together to share laughter, food, and ideas, as well as to help each other in times in need and hardship. And you can create such a community in your life through Light of the Eternal One.

Creating community with Light of the Eternal One can take many forms. It can be as simple as you performing situational treatments to manifest a solid community of good friends in your life, who may or may not be interested in energy work or Light of the Eternal One. Or, it can involve creating a community of dedicated healers and energy workers who assist each other on a regular basis, while also doing good works for the surrounding community as well by offering free treatments or sending healing light to helping the planet. In fact, most people belong to several different communities at the same time. Each community represents an aspect of that person's interests, be it cooking, writing, art, politics, religion, nature, or other subjects that draw people together. With Light of the Eternal One you can both create new communities in your life as well as deepen the relationship and quality of the ones you are already part of.

To do this, begin by performing situational treatments on creating more and better community in your life. Simply place your hands in the proper position for this treatment, pinkies touching and palms facing the sky. Then, imagine you are holding a miniature you in the palm of your hands, surrounded by people who love and care about you, people who you can share your interests with, and who share common interests with each other. Even sense as you are visualizing this, those lines of Divine light that connect each person, feeling them deepen and radiate the purest expression of Divine love. Now, flow Light of the Eternal One through your hands into this image, feeling it strengthen the sense of community in your life. As the energy flows, you may sense things you should do, or conversations you need to have, to help make this level of community a reality in your life. Listen to these, and act upon them when the time is right.

If you perform this treatment on a regular basis, you will see the overall level of community in your life deepen and grow. But know as well that not only can you grow the sense of community in your life by performing situational treatments, but that you can also create community in your life by bringing Light of the Eternal One into those friendships and relationships where it feels appropriate. Not all of your friends may be into energy work, or find it as something that is of interest to them. But for those that do, hosting a regular Light of the Eternal One healing circle is a wonderful way to create a community in your life that supports the work you are doing from this book. And if it seems like you want more than just friends to be part of this group, you can always post fliers around the neighborhood or use other creative ways to let people know you are starting a regular healing circle using Light of the Eternal One. If people want to join but have no experience, you can either share this book with them, or teach them yourself if you have received the teaching empowerment from Chapter 23.

This healing circle can be much more than just people gathering to send Divine light to each other and to the planet. It can be a joyful celebration of each other and each person's life in the group. When creating such a group, know that you are creating it with right intention, that you are sending out this call to the universe from a place of love. You can have it be celebratory in tone, by making it a potluck, and having celebratory music playing as people arrive. Think out these steps in detail before the event, and embellish them with as much love as possible, performing Light of the Eternal One situational treatments on each step if necessary.

A general flow of such a circle may include blessing each person as they arrive with a Light of the Eternal One basic treatment, which will almost certainly create a blissful and euphoric tone from the start. Then, as a group, bless any food that is part of the potluck with Light of the Eternal One by performing a group treatment on the food. Note that this is a celebration, and as you are honoring the food you are about to communally share in eating, you are also seeing those Divine lines of light move out from the food to also honor the farmer, the grocer, and everyone who has been part of the journey of this food being present for this group at this point in time. Hold this treatment for five minutes, and let it resonate through each molecule of the communal meal. Then, joyfully share the meal without any agendas. This portion of the gathering should come from the heart and not be filled with too many obligatory concerns. The meal itself will deepen the connection between all of you, and your connection to the Divine, through the blessing of it with Light of the Eternal One.

Give time for the meal to take its course, and when it comes to a fruitful end, take some time to send Light of the Eternal One treatments to situations requested by individuals in the group. These situations can be about personal issues in their lives, or about community healings or planetary healings. Again, I recommend letting the agenda flow freely, as you want everyone to feel free in the expression of what they want to see worked on as a group. When everyone has had the opportunity to have the group send energy to their concerns, send a final blessing to the group itself, to deepen its true purpose of bringing joy and light to all who are part of it. Then, give thanks to each other and thanks to the Divine as a final closing.

Obviously, there can be many variations on the above suggestions for having a regular Light of the Eternal One group to help create more community in your life. Feel empowered to personalize the above suggested outline to suit your own needs and concerns. For there is no one way to do this, no central authority saying how it must be. Have fun. Be kind, to yourself and others. And know that there are others of like mind who want to share this work with you. That is all you really need to know.

30

The Snowman Melting From the Inside Out

What happens to you when you really begin to take on Light of the Eternal One as part of your life? Whether you teach it regularly to others, or simply perform the basic treatment on yourself each day, you are engaging a light that will deepen your experience of the Divine, and your experience of life. Notice the changes you may have already experienced simply from the empowerments you have received through this book. If you have kept a regular journal on this process, you have the facts before you.

The real purpose of Light of the Eternal One is to continuously peel away that separation consciousness that makes us often feel alone, afraid, despondent, and also creates dis-ease in our lives. When that sense of separation begins to be peeled away, you begin to see things from a new perspective, and this impacts not only your perception of the world but also how you engage the world. You become more friendly toward others, even those you do not know. You feel lighter and happier. Eventually, especially if you do the work geared toward piercing the veil of Maya, you will begin to notice a deep sense of spacious within. And if you try to find yourself within that spaciousness, you will not find anyone there but something much greater than yourself, a presence of which you are created. For some, that can be a source of confusion, as the ego tries to find itself in the huge, empty peace of the Divine that now shines within you. That peace is free of dramas, addictions, the fuel that is the ego's greatest strength. It is simply emptiness, pure potential, undifferentiated consciousness that is presence without an *I*.

The analogy I like to use to explain this is that of the snowman melting from the inside out. First of all, the snowman is really only a conglomeration of water, the sacred water that flows through all life on this planet in some form or another. And if the snowman was conscious and aware of its true nature, which is water, then it may not think of itself as in any way separate from anything else. For there is water in the trees, the surrounding vegetation of the lawn on which this snowman exists. And yet, if we give this snowman a human ego, it would think of itself as separate. It would not feel its connection with the other beings that are also mostly made of water. It would simply think of itself as this form, a form that some may call a snowman.

But if this snowman had a way of accessing its true identity, of seeing itself as water, and knowing the water essence of itself, perhaps it could make the ice inside itself turn back into water, so that it could know its true self. Let's say that through meditation, or energy work, the snowman now had the capacity to slowly begin making the ice within turn back into water. Then, the snowman would slowly begin to melt from the inside out.

At first, the snowman may only notice some interesting sensations. Or, it may feel nothing at all, except a sense of peace now and then from the experience of the water returning to its true form, which helps the snowman know what it truly is made of, what its real essence is about. Let's say that after a week, the snowman has a space inside where there is no snow at all, nor even water, but simply spaciousness. Yet this too is part of what the snowman truly is: space, just as all of us have an area of space within us.

The snowman then begins to understand that it is space as well, and that this space holds a place of deep peace—and even joy—because it is what most of the universe actually is, only space. But, if the snowman is attached to its idea of being a snowman, the way many of us are attached to the ego, it will feel a great deal of confusion at this point because the *I* that it thinks it is made of is dissolving. Yet, as this dissolving continues and the snowman continues to melt from the inside out, there becomes more and more space, more peace on the inside of the snowman if the snowman decides to be aware of it.

And if someone were passing by, and could not tell that the snowman had melted some on the inside, they would not necessarily think any changes had happened to this snowman. But the snowman, feeling the spaciousness and the reconnection with the water that are its true nature, may simply begin to feel peaceful, even joyous all the time, because it is now understanding it is made of something greater than what it originally imagined itself to be.

And soon, if the snowman melts fast enough, the changes on the outside may also begin to show. The children who walk past the snowman each day may feel a sadness that they have lost an imaginary friend, just as sometimes in real life those around us become saddened when in fact we are making beautiful changes in our life. Because they only see what is happening on the outside, that the form of the snowman—which is equal to our ego—is dissolving. And that which they could cling on to, the idea of a snowman, is now becoming something more open; the spaciousness of the Divine.

Eventually, the snowman will melt entirely. And if the identification is with the form of the snowman, then there will be sadness and confusion. But if the identification is with the true essence of that snowman, the water of which it was made and the space wherein its form was contained, things eternal, then there is actually a sense of deeper peace and joy.

I use this analogy because the spiritual journey can often feel like the snowman melting from the inside out. At first, no one—not the snowman, nor the friends of the snowman—wants the snowman to dissolve. This is because they all identify with its form, not its true essence. And yet, if the snowman begins to understand that it is water and space, not the form, then there is simply a sense of freedom and peace that comes with dissolving, and no attachment to being a snowman at all.

The more you use Light of the Eternal One, the more you may begin to feel like a snowman melting from the inside out. You will deepen your relationship to the true Divine aspect of yourself, which is like the water from the story and is that of which you are truly made. Everything else is simply projection and ego. As people pass, they see something they call a snowman, either an ugly snowman or laughing snowman or scary snowman, whatever their projections might be. When, in fact, it is just water that has changed shape for a period of time, to be amused at what it can do.

Once the water knows itself as water, it becomes more fluid, and becomes part of a never-ending journey, a journey much greater than the life of a snowman. The water knows itself as connected to the lakes, the rivers, the oceans, and all the life that is made of water. And too, the space that was on the inside of the snowman, if it had consciousness, would know itself as the same space that exists between stars and planets, and something that is much greater than the snowman. So as the snowman melts from the inside out, these more real aspects of its essence are liberated and become free.

So too it is with our egos. Think of the ego as the snowman, and that once the ego dies or melts, the true essence of the self is liberated. What Light of the Eternal One does is melt that snowman from the inside out. If you have been practicing regular treatments on a daily basis, you may feel that spaciousness now inside you, or you may feel an inkling of it from time to time. And the more you work with Light of the Eternal One, the more that spaciousness inside you will grow, the more you will know yourself as part of the greater *We* that are the stars, the fish, the oceans, the rocks, the mountains, the rest of humanity, even the angels and other beings we cannot even see. Melt back into that greater *We*, like the snowman who became water and returned to the sea.

31

Metaphors in Consciousness

Contained in this chapter are a series of metaphors, meditations, and aphorism to help deepen your consciousness into Light of the Eternal One. Each paragraph can be read separately from the rest, as each one is a self-contained doorway toward deepening your consciousness into this wonderful energy called Light of the Eternal One. You can always come back to this chapter to reinforce your connection to this energy. And though this chapter is not meant as a replacement for performing the actual treatments, it can offer sustenance to those who crave more than just energy, those who want a foundation of work that will stimulate the mind in ways that are perhaps difficult to articulate when actually performing treatments on yourself. Please read the following words and rest in the embrace they offer. Then, read them a second time while simultaneously performing the basic treatment on yourself.

Drink from the light that is you before you became yourself. It is pure presence, pure essence unfolding. For if the Divine gave charge to the atoms that made you with a breath of light, then you are too of that same breath. See this breath now flowing through your own hands.

Empty into that which is held in your hands. Be stunned at who you are: a creature created with Divine intention. Suck upon the light beyond form, bringing it back into form. There, in the meeting of this place, exists eternity.

A wave of light comes from that unknown place, much as a wave from the ocean rises up to wash your mind back into freedom. Let it take you, for it is all you have ever been.

Bless your head first, then your eyes, then the wisdom that abounds from you. Stare into that love, which is nothing more than universe.

The natural curve of space time is Buddha smiling.

Willfully expose yourself to the journey inward, as if a bell is ringing that calls you to feast with the Divine.

Place your hands upon your head, and know that the universe is melting.

All craving ceases, opening into true joy.

We often realize ourselves only after death. Imagine you have already died, and then live your life with freedom.

As if each molecule of your brain is singing the many names of the Divine, this is how the light touches you.

The light exists before existence, therefore it is always without end. It comes from everywhere and the place that is beyond everywhere. It comes from all time, and beyond time. In resting your hands on anything, you bring all eternity with you when flowing this light.

Imagine the joy of the Divine, seeping between each second, announcing itself through each pore of your body. This is the purpose of Light of the Eternal One.

Go into the wilderness of your soul, and take note of every fearful creature you encounter. All of them are only seeking love. Feed them this light, and these creatures shall all be as friends to you.

Hold in your hands every encounter in time, in every second of every life where you felt lost from the One. Then flow Light of the Eternal One to fill the gaps, so that you may remember yourself.

Between each vertebra of your spine is the sound of peace. Let your spine sing to you.

If each finger on your hand were an angel, what might they say when holding your head. Sometimes, when flowing the light, I hear the wisdom of these angels.

Light legislates freedom. It is the ultimate law without words.

Be creative with your endeavors in using this light. Touch where your imagination leads you. And then some.

Explode beyond the pages of who you imagine yourself to be. Eternal is your nature, so follow it as the light moves within you.

Behind your eyelids is the dream of time. Where do your eyes go when that dream awakens?

Sacredly touch the now, and feel it being held in your hands like a feather. Bring all the universe into its awareness with the light.

Meditate on the euphoria you feel after being embraced by the Light of the Eternal One. Where does this euphoria come from? Is it you remembering the moment when God and Goddess were making love to create all that you have ever been?

Imagine the laughter of the Divine echoing through your hands. This is the light I mention.

Who is the greater We, that Us beyond us? If all is One, how can there be anything else? Turn the puzzle like a Rubik's Cube, and suddenly all is *aha!*

All the nothing I have ever known amounts to this moment. How can anything be more precious than that?

All of the universe is a banana flower silently opening in your hands.

32

The Lesson of Simplicity

I am reminded of one of the first students I had when teaching this to the staff at Omega Institute. It was when I still referred to this work as *Om Blessing*. At the time, a woman named Lyn was one of two students who attended my first class. She learned the basic treatment, which was all that I taught at the time, since other techniques with this work had yet to be developed. And though she did not study with me in any other way that season at Omega, I watched her grow spiritually over the next six months.

She was doing other work on herself as well that season, so I did not think to even ask if the new sense of happiness and confidence that she exuded was at all related to her taking my class in the early part of the season. From time to time, however, she would come up and let me know that she did the work daily, again calling it Om Blessing.

Yet on the final day of the season at Omega Institute, she came up to me and told me how much the Om Blessing meant to her, how much it had

ENERGY HEALING FOR EVERYONE

changed her life. She expressed such a deep sense of gratitude that I felt called to honor it by writing this book, knowing that there are many other people like Lyn, who may never do anything with this energy other than perform the basic treatment on a daily basis, and that even in staying committed to this one daily act, their lives can profoundly change.

It is with this deep sense of simplicity that Lyn showed me that we can all grow and learn by simply doing this one small act each day. We do not need any deep, esoteric knowledge, though that is fine if you have it. The only thing we really need is the consistent act each day of wanting to be just a little bit closer to the Divine, to move deeper into that relationship on a daily basis.

This book possibly could have been only one page long, and still carried the essence of what is needed to understand this work. In this book, there are techniques to expand upon your knowledge of Light of the Eternal One, as well as empowerments for the basic and teacher levels. Such things are worth knowing, and will help this light spread faster to others who will benefit from using it. But, the basic treatment is truly all that you need to change your life. Even if you do not have time for the situational/ relationship treatments, or to work on piercing the veil of Maya, or intentionally creating a deeper sense of community through this work, the Light of the Eternal One basic treatment can change your life.

33

The Divine Rainbow
of Light

There are many forms of Divine light that are now available to humanity, and though these lights all come from the same Divine source, each carries a slightly different vibration and function. I often use the analogy of these lights being part of a rainbow. The source of a rainbow's light is always the sun, and yet each band of light that exists in that rainbow is different, and each can impact our consciousness in different ways. Just as the colors blue and red both exist in the rainbow, they are still distinctively separate bands of light. Red has a more energizing quality and blue is more relaxing. And yet, as part of the rainbow, the source of both red and blue is the light of the sun.

I mention this because too often I hear some people who are not that familiar with energy work think that it all must be the same, that Reiki, Magical Awakening, Rei Ju, Joh Rei, and other forms of Divine light are all just the same thing since they all come from the Divine. And similarly, I have also known practitioners of one form of light try to disregard the importance and effectiveness of other bands of Divine light that are essentially part of this same Divine rainbow. In a strange way, some practitioners get territorial and protective, as if they have to prove their light is the best light of all.

Light of the Eternal One is simply one of these many lights from the Divine. It is one that is simple and easy to learn, and therefore will appeal to a great number of people. But it is not necessarily in any other way the be-all and end-all of energy work. It is simply one band of light in an amazing rainbow being offered to us now by the Divine. My purpose for mentioning this is for two reasons.

First, I dearly hope that those who practice the work of this book practice tolerance and openness toward other energy forms and those practitioners who work with those forms. A disheartening part of my own journey as an energy worker has been when I hear teachers from one modality attack other modalities, saying things to stir up fear in their students to discourage them from trying out these other forms of Divine light. This behavior reminds me of the kind of fanaticism we see in the world among certain religions, where there is a sense that unless you are practicing *our way*, you must somehow be misguided. Such behavior is nonsense, especially when it comes from a segment of the population that so often proclaims wanting to usher in a new era of an enlightened age.

I have heard of this type of behavior taking various forms, such as a well-known student of one lineage being referred to at one point as enlightened by a teacher, only to have that enlightenment disclaimed and discredited years later by the same teacher when the student discovers their own modality of energy work. Also, I have even known the question to arise from a dear friend who I deeply love and respect, who once asked me if Reiki spirit guides would get angry at a Reiki practitioner for using other forms of energy work. As much as I love and respect my friend, such questions make me wonder how the world of energy workers can really be so divided. What is this core issue that makes us want to disparage other forms of healing work in favor of our own? Sometimes, I think the reason is based on a fear of competition. But often, I think it is simply that we are conditioned to think in terms of there is only one right way to do things. We see this in religion, politics, and so many other areas of human life.

My plea, then, is that all who read this book please respect and honor all forms of this Divine rainbow, be it Reiki, Renewal, Magical Awakening, or some other form of healing light from the Divine. And, similarly, my hope is that those who practice traditions other than this one will not disparage it simply because it is new, unknown, and may have a different appeal than other, more established forms of energy healing.

We no longer need to live with a patriarchal worldview that assumes there is only room for one ultimate authority at the top. This view has not served the world kindly in the realms of politics, economics, race, gender, or religion. Nor does it serve us as energy healers. The practice of tolerance and acceptance must begin with us if we have a greater desire to change the world and make it a better place, as most energy practitioners often claim.

So, follow the path than works for you, regardless of what it may be. But, please show tolerance of other forms of energy healing. I find that having access to a number of modalities has been very beneficial. My own preference is to learn as many lines of Divine light as possible, to give me greater access to the Divine rainbow. But that is simply my own preference. There are wonderful healers who practice only one form, and will never stray from that form. And this is fine. Again, the key must always be tolerance, even if you do not understand the other form, even when some of its principles or techniques may not appeal to you, please refrain from judgment. For that energy form may be the very spiritual medicine that some soul, or group of souls, desperately needs.

This also leads to a second point I wish to make, which is a request that those who use this work refrain from trying to turn me, or themselves, into anyone's guru. As one who works where many wonderful spiritual teachers offer workshops each year, an ongoing disappointment has been when people put others on pedestals, or when individuals put themselves on a pedestal. It is a trap, both for the student and the teacher when this happens. It is a trap for the student because they project their own power and innate abilities on to the teacher instead of taking responsibility for it themselves. And it is a trap for the teacher, who then has to live up to some whitewashed, inauthentic image of what everyone thinks a guru or spiritual teacher is supposed to be.

Light of the Eternal One is simply a Divine light that is part of a greater Divine rainbow of healing lights. Because I research energy and have discovered new techniques that involve using my higher self to be able to probe for new energies that are part of this Divine rainbow, I was able to gain access to Light of the Eternal One. But all credit for this happening goes to the Divine, not me.

I may have an understanding of how this light functions, and be blessed with the empowerments I was given to be able to share this light with others. But that does not make me all-knowing or all-wise. Nor does it make anyone who practices this work have such attributes. The power is in the light itself, which is now in your hands if you have chosen to activate it through the chants in this book. It belongs to the Divine and everyone, and is meant for creating the greater good in all of us, to lift us all to a higher plane, where we know how deeply connected we are, and how loved by the Divine we are.

This light is free and democratic. And it is my hope that all who share it will see themselves as equals, neither above one another, nor above those practitioners of other forms of healing light, nor above those who practice no form of energy healing at all. For this light is designed to help you know the greater *We*, and in that *We* there is no fear of others, no competition with others, no need to put yourself above or below anyone else.

And always know, the real answer has little to do with these words, and is always now held in your hands as Light of the Eternal One.